T0347199

Essential Aloneness

Essential Aloneness

Rome Lectures on DW Winnicott

CHRISTOPHER BOLLAS

OXFORD
UNIVERSITY PRESS

OXFORD
UNIVERSITY PRESS

Oxford University Press is a department of the University of Oxford. It furthers
the University's objective of excellence in research, scholarship, and education
by publishing worldwide. Oxford is a registered trade mark of Oxford University
Press in the UK and certain other countries.

Published in the United States of America by Oxford University Press
198 Madison Avenue, New York, NY 10016, United States of America.

© Christopher Bollas 2024

Library of Congress Cataloging-in-Publication Data
Names: Bollas, Christopher, author.
Title: Essential aloneness : Rome lectures on DW Winnicott / Christopher Bollas.
Description: New York, NY : Oxford University Press, [2024] |
Includes bibliographical references and index. |
Identifiers: LCCN 2023017306 (print) | LCCN 2023017307 (ebook) |
ISBN 9780197683880 (hardback) | ISBN 9780197683903 (epub) |
ISBN 9780197683910
Subjects: LCSH: Winnicott, D. W. (Donald Woods), 1896–1971. |
Infant psychology—Philosophy. | Developmental psychology. |
Solitude—Psychological aspects.
Classification: LCC BF719.5 .B48 2024 (print) | LCC BF719.5 (ebook) |
DDC 155 .42/2—dc23/eng/20230612
LC record available at https://lccn.loc.gov/2023017306
LC ebook record available at https://lccn.loc.gov/2023017307

DOI: 10.1093/oso/9780197683880.001.0001

Printed by Sheridan Books, Inc., United States of America

Contents

Introduction

These lectures were presented in 1986 and 1987 to staff, students, and others at the Istituto di Neuropsichiatria Infantile at the University of Rome, where I was visiting professor of psychoanalysis in the child psychotherapy training programme.

The Istituto was referred to by both locals and visitors as 'Via Sabelli' after the street where it lived. I was one of several British psychoanalysts, including Francis Tustin and Paula Heimann, who were regular visitors in the 1970s and 1980s. The British connection began through links established by Dr Andreas Giannakoulas, who had trained at the British Society. The heart and soul of this programme were rooted in the genius of Dr Adriano Giannotti, who assembled a remarkable staff that included many psychoanalysts.

The Italians had taken to Winnicott early on—in the 1950s—largely due to the intellectual sponsorship of Eugenio and Renata Gaddini, who knew Winnicott and were involved intermittently at Via Sabelli. I delivered the lectures presented here to an audience that was not simply literate in Winnicott but *using* him. The areas of his thinking that I selected were particularly relevant to clinical work, and I wanted to address questions that linked theory to practice. The topics focused on questions that arose out of his writings, issues that seemed to be left lingering in time. Winnicott simply did not have enough of it (who does?) to cover all the bases. So we discussed subjects such as how to facilitate true self in sessions, how to identify a breakdown in the true self, and how to address patterns established between mother and infant.

Although we had been studying Winnicott's writings for years, Giannotti decided we should dedicate some years to identifying

Essential Aloneness. Christopher Bollas, Oxford University Press. © Christopher Bollas 2024.
DOI: 10.1093/oso/9780197683880.001.0001

crucial clinical axioms that would help clinicians change their practice. We were all inspired by Winnicott, but what could we do differently in our work, having internalized his views?

Our days began with a morning clinical presentation. This would be open to those doing the child psychotherapy training as well as members of the staff and other interested mental health professionals. The clinical discussion would reverberate through the day and would inevitably inform the afternoon lecture, which was also open to people admitted to the series as guests. On Fridays I would give an evening talk that was open to the public.

The clinical presentations are not reproduced here, although I do include fragments of our discussion of some cases as well as questions from the audience. Often, I would find myself adjusting the next lecture on the basis of these questions. This way I could adapt to the audience's interests, and they became a vital part of this collaboration. Those included in the present text will help give the reader a feel of the audience and its participation.

The lectures presented here vary in length for several reasons. Ideas we had grappled with on previous occasions—such as discussion of the true self—might be covered in less depth, and some lectures were inadequately transcribed or material was lost. It was decided, nonetheless, to include these shortened lectures and to allow them to stand as-is. However tempting it was to step in and expand them, doing so would violate my commitment to leaving the lectures unedited. Finally, the lectures would often end rather abruptly on an evocative topic, a strategy intended to generate ideas in the students. This was best accomplished by leaving them to their own thoughts.

In editing these lectures some thirty-five years after they were given, I have made only minor syntactical changes. I do not comment on the talks, thus sparing myself and the reader intrusions from the future.

These are not by any means intended to be comprehensive lectures on Winnicott. There are by now many books on him, including a new standard edition of his collected works published by Oxford University Press. Each of these volumes has an extensive introduction that places Winnicott's work in an historical context. These commentaries are invaluable when tracking the evolution of his ideas, which were continually evolving and changing.

There are many fine essays on Winnicott's work that bear witness to this 'use of an object'. For me, Adam Phillips' short book on Winnicott is still the best introduction to his thinking, and Jan Abrams' remarkable dictionary of Winnicott provides the student with a thorough discussion of many of his ideas.

Readers familiar with Winnicott's writing will note that the lectures also, invariably, wander off into discussions of issues of particular interest to me, including concepts—the transformational object, the unthought known, subject relations theory—that were circulating in my own writings at the time. Those not familiar with my work may wish to study Sarah Nettleton's book *The Metapsychology of Christopher Bollas: an Introduction.*[1]

Over four decades of visits to Rome, from 1977 to 2018, I was graciously supported by many people. I wish to thank especially Vincenzo Bonaminio, Marco-Lombardo Ridice, Anna Bouvet-Chagall, Elena Natale, Anna and Peter Hobart, and Giuliana de Astis.

I owe particular gratitude to Daniela Molina, my indefatigable Italian translator.

My thanks go to Daniel Schwartz, Medical Director of the Austen Riggs Center in Stockbridge, Massachusetts, where I was Director of Education in the middle 1980s, for supporting these lectures at a long distance. Betty Homich, my secretary at the Austen Riggs Center, worked tirelessly to transcribe them from tapes to page.

Thanks also to Arne Jemstedt of Stockholm and Ed Corrigan of New York, who read these lectures and urged me to publish them

---

[1] London, Routledge (2017).

when I was very unsure of the wisdom of that prospect, and to Sarah Nettleton, whose editorial comments and assistance are invaluable. Lastly I thank Suzanne Bollas, for the lengthy task of transferring the typed version to modern computer.

Winnicott Books Cited

Human Nature. London, Free Association Books,1988. (**HN**)

Deprivation and Delinquency. London and New York, Tavistock, 1984. (**DD**)

The Maturational Processes and the Facilitating Environment. London, Hogarth, 1972. (**MP**)

Through Paediatrics to Psycho-Analysis. London, Hogarth, 1975. (**TP**)

Playing and Reality. London, Tavistock, 1971. (**PR**)

1

Aloneness

Today I have brought with me Winnicott's 'private' book[1], which we are going to publish for the first time next year. As you know, he wrote many papers and essays that were collected into volumes, but in fact it was a secret that he kept to himself and his wife that he had been writing this book from 1954 until his death in 1971. He called it 'The Primer', and he would often dip into it before he gave a talk on the radio or elsewhere.

I will begin by reading from 'The Primer', as there are fascinating sections on his musings on aloneness—the aloneness of the predependent infant—which bears on a concept that I term the unthought known: something that is *known* but that has not yet been *thought*. I am interested in the way in which an infant internalizes experiences which, although not mentally represented, are stored in the ego and become a form of knowledge. Winnicott asks: 'What is the state of the human individual as the being emerges out of not being?' (HN131)—a question that Heidegger might pose, but in this case it is offered by a psychoanalyst-paediatrician, who observes infants emerging from a state prior to existence. Winnicott continues:

> Except at the start there is never exactly reproduced this funda-
> mental and inherent aloneness. Nevertheless throughout the life
> of an individual there continues a fundamental unalterable and
> inherent aloneness, along with which goes unawareness of the
> conditions that are essential to the state of aloneness. (HN132)

---

[1] Now published as *Human Nature* (London, Free Associations, 1988).

Essential Aloneness. Christopher Bollas, Oxford University Press. © Christopher Bollas 2024.
DOI: 10.1093/oso/9780197683880.003.0001

He describes a condition which must be maintained by the mother's act of provision, that supports positive aloneness. If this aloneness is not permitted, something is lost. Aloneness is an essential state.

> Most of what is commonly said and felt about death is about this first state *before aliveness*, where aloneness is a fact and long before dependence is encountered. The life of an individual is an interval between two states of unaliveness. The first of these, out of which aliveness arises, colours ideas people have about the second death. (HN132)

We could say that the foetus evolves from unaliveness to aloneness—a transition, remembered in our unconscious, that informs our view of life and death. We may view death as an inevitable return to aloneness, or we may regard it as a horrid, chaotic annihilation. Winnicott suggests that our relation to death is based on the transition from unaliveness to aloneness. Here he cites Freud:

> Freud spoke of the inorganic state from which each individual emerges and to which each returns, and from this idea he formulated his idea of the Life and Death instincts. There is evidence of Freud's genius in his putting forward this obvious fact and implying that a truth lay hidden in it. (HN132)

He continues:

> . . . this state arising before dependence can be recognized, dependence being on absolute dependability; this state being much prior to instinct, and still more removed from capacity for guilt. What could be more natural than that this state that has been experienced should be reclaimed in explanation of the unknowable death that comes after life? (HN133)

The idea that aloneness is prior to dependence and instinct makes an important distinction. The fundamental nature of being precedes experience of the object and the urgent demand of instincts. Being precedes object dependence, object relatedness, and instinctual life.

Being precedes existence!

This brings to mind Freud's statement that instincts make a demand upon the mind for work. Object relations theory added that the object world makes a similar demand. We may now add another dimension—part of the unthought known—if we conclude that aloneness also makes a demand upon a curious mind for work.

Winnicott maintains that a good birth is based on an illusion: the infant's assumption that his aggression creates birth. There is a crucial link between being and aggression. Aggression translates being into aliveness and it is vital to the formation of the individual. 'If on the other hand there is no aggressive element,' he writes,

> in the primitive love impulse, but only anger at frustration, and if therefore the change from ruthlessness to concern is of no importance, then it is necessary to look round for an alternative theory of aggression, and then the Death Instinct must be re-examined. (HN134)

Winnicott writes about a capacity for experience which is based upon foetal existence. He maintains that whereas a post-mature infant shows evidence of having been too long in the womb, the premature infant seems to have a poor capacity for experience as a human being. The foetus stores experience, and therefore there is in all human beings memory of foetal life.

We are familiar with Winnicott's concept of continuity of being, which is the condition necessary for the successful evolution of the true self, and how he distinguishes continuity of being from reaction to impingement. Although the environment is very important, impingement in itself is not intrinsically traumatic. It is not the environment that creates a trauma, but the infant's *reaction* to impingement that can prove to be traumatic.

Winnicott believes that environmental influences start very early in the intrauterine state, and bias the extent to which the infant will either go out to seek experience or choose to withdraw from the world. Before birth, the infant becomes accustomed to interruptions of being, so by the time of birth itself the infant has already become accustomed to impingement: the intrusions of pressure, temperature, sound, and so much more.

In foetal life there is preparation for birth, and ordinary impingements are essential for a 'good birth.' At full term there is already a human being in the womb, and that human being is capable of experiencing and accumulating body memories of these experiences and of organizing defences in relation to certain challenges. Foetuses come to their birth with differing capacities for what Winnicott calls 'the great changeover' from being unborn to being born.

Normal birth has three features. In the first place, it is a gross interruption of the continuity of being, but the infant has already accumulated experiences of impingement and therefore is ready. Secondly, the infant has built up memories of sensations and impulses that become self-phenomena, since they belong to a period of being, rather than to a period of reacting. Since the sense of self emerges through continuity of being, the foetus is already experiencing self, and this sense is an organization that will be useful in negotiating the trauma of birth. The third feature of a normal birth is that it should be neither premature nor prolonged. Winnicott makes many references to the traumatic effects of these two eventualities.

As I mentioned earlier, he believes that the infant has a sensory illusion of creating his own birth. So he says that we must postulate a birth that is a good enough birth from the *infant's* point of view. It is not excessively impinging; it is something produced by the infant's impulses to movement and change, which spring directly out of the infant's aliveness.

Winnicott emphasizes the transition from unaliveness to aliveness, and a part of the theory of true self brings us to a further distinction: between being and aliveness. Aliveness is affiliated with aggression and movement. Being and aliveness are compatible, but they are not the same. We could say that an infant who 'thought' it was simply being that created his birth would be a severely disturbed infant indeed. It is possible that some narcissistic disturbances can be traced to the sense that pure being is sufficient, and that alive existence should simply emerge out of this pure being.

What about the experience of time?

Some babies are not born on time, and Winnicott believes that as a result we may find a clinical base for certain individuals' intellectual interest in time and the development of what he calls a 'timing sense'. There are some people who, if they must go to an airport, have to get there three hours before the plane leaves. Others will arrive five minutes before departure; and then, of course, there are those who arrive after it has gone. We cannot study whether there is a relation between prematurity or prolongation of birth and the application of a sense of timing, but it is an interesting idea.

In 'The Primer' Winnicott recommends that the infant be allowed to have immediate contact with the mother: to lie naked on the mother's belly. This is necessary because the newborn needs the continuity of reconnecting with the mother's breathing and with the maternal heartbeat. Infants have a common breathing rate (one breath every four heart beats), and Winnicott suggests that this common breath is a fundamental core experience. The infant then plays with his own breathing rate, making cross rhythms between breathing and heart rate, both in himself and in relation to the mother.

In the following passage, Winnicott talks about a primary chaos out of which we all emerge:

> It is not necessary to postulate an original state of chaos. Chaos is a concept which carries with it the idea of order; and darkness too is not there at the beginning, since darkness implies light. At the beginning before each individual creates the world anew there is a simple state of being, and a dawning awareness of continuity of being and of continuity of existence in time. (HN135)

He continues:

> Chaos becomes meaningful exactly as there is to be discerned some kind of order. It represents an alternative to order, and by the time chaos itself can be sensed by the individual it has already become a kind of order, a state which may become organized in defence against anxiety associated with the order. (HN135)

Let me tell you what I think he means. Of course we understand that if the chaos caused by impingement becomes too much, then a quantity of chaos is internalized as a part of the infant's self. It becomes an alternative to order at the time when the infant is beginning to sense the difference between order and chaos.

Think for a moment of the borderline personality, in which chaos can be used defensively against order. The borderline patient's intense, frothy, chaotic thinking can be a defence against the anxiety of the ordered structure of guilt.

To return to Winnicott:

> Chaos gathers to itself new meaning in relation to the order that is called integration. . . . Each form of chaos contributes to the chaos that belongs to the subsequent stages, and recovery from

chaos in an early stage gives a positive contribution to recovering from chaos later. (HN135–6)

We see again how chaotic experience, resulting from effects of impingement, is necessary to the formation of emotional reality. We may now make distinctions between being and aliveness and emotional reality, which links up with psyche. We can see that something like chaos is necessary for a good enough birth. No doubt there will be a degree of chaos in the environment which can only result in a chaotic defensive state in the individual. This can have a result difficult to distinguish clinically from the mental defect that belongs to poverty of brain tissue. The defect results, in this case, in a permanent hold-up of development that dates from a very early stage. The chaos of the inner world is a much later phenomenon.

2

Living with . . . (M)other

Let's begin by thinking about pregnancy. Amongst other things, pregnancy is a psychobiological learning experience in which the mother gradually becomes rather helpless. This helplessness is not simply psychological: in the third trimester she may be so heavy that it is difficult to get up from a chair. She may find it difficult to maintain her balance while walking downstairs. Sleep is difficult, and she may wake several times during the night just as somebody else will soon be waking in the early hours.

Pregnancy prepares the mother for identification with the new-born baby, so a mother who feels helpless may actually be preparing to be a good enough mother. Feeling vulnerable, tearful, and overly dependent on her partner may make her more attuned to the infantile state of being.

We can link the multiple functions of pregnancy with Winnicott's theory of 'primary maternal preoccupation'. This is a special state of the mother that refers to a mother's particular concentration on her baby, in the weeks before and after its birth.

If she has had a good enough pregnancy, if she has gradually been learning what it is to be an infant, then the arrival of the baby completes her own infantile regression. The birth coincides with the emergence of the infant part of the mother, and for two or three weeks there is an intense identification with the baby.

It is important in understanding the mother's capacity for 'holding' the infant to assess her own capacity, during pregnancy, to make use of her partner or husband for holding. Can a pregnant mother seek out her husband and close friends and grow into some form of caretaking? In cases of puerperal psychosis, the new

Essential Aloneness. Christopher Bollas, Oxford University Press. © Christopher Bollas 2024.
DOI: 10.1093/oso/9780197683880.003.0002

mother may have been so preoccupied with the autistic features of pregnancy that she was unable to seek or find in the husband support for dependent existence. Thus she can have no experience of recovery from dependence, based on the facilitating work and presence of the other.

Many times when discussing what he calls 'the holding environment', Winnicott emphasizes the fact of dependence. It was his view that this fact had not matriculated into the theory of psychoanalysis after Freud's time. In other words the infant is truly dependent on the mother, not only for his physical existence but also for the quality of his life.

Winnicott was in many respects critical of the Kleinian implication that the mother is significant only insofar as she exists for the baby as a creation of his projection. Of course she is not simply the figment of the child's phantasies. She exists, has her own personality, and organizes her own idiom of maternal care which has an ego-structuring effect on her baby. From Winnicott's point of view, the quality of her care is crucial to the emotional well-being of the infant.

One of the mother's tasks in sustaining the holding environment is to maintain an undisrupted sense of time. This maintaining of time allows the infant maximum experiencing of his own being. Continuity of being is the dynamic thread vital to the evolution of self. In order to maintain this, the mother must allow the infant to create the illusion that he creates his world. So a good enough mother knows when the infant is hungry and she presents the breast at the moment when the baby imagines it, as if his instinctual urges both form the image of the breast and create its reality. From the infant's subjective point of view, therefore, it is *as if* he has created reality, but in fact it depends on the actions of the external mother.

By generating illusion the mother gives the infant an experience of omnipotence, which permits him to 'gather together' the details of external life. This gathering together of experiences is crucial to the infant's capacity to engage with reality without his 'continuity of being' being disturbed by it. Imagine a mother who does not maintain the infant's sense of continuity because she is always late in presenting the breast. Maybe she believes it is wrong to give in to the baby's demands, and that it is good for the baby to wait for a few minutes before a feed. This infant will not have an experience of omnipotence nor a sense of his creation of the object. Instead he may experience an inner annihilation of being.

Winnicott disagreed with Anna Freud when he said the infant's need for the breast is not fundamentally an instinctual need. In the early weeks of life it is not a question of gratification or frustration. These are concepts that apply to instinctual life; they are not appropriate when it is a question of need. A need is either met or it is not. A need that is not met can result in an experience of annihilation of being. Those of you who have had babies or have seen small babies in a state of annihilation understand what we are talking about. It is not a question of frustration or gratification, which are organized experiences. An infant whose need is not met descends into chaos.

In some ways we could say that one of the differences between the schizophrenic and the borderline is that the schizophrenic has organized himself against any experience, because experiences of annihilation are too devastating. The borderline maintains intense object cathexes, and continues to have repeated experiences of annihilation of being, because this psychic texture is the shadow of the mother.

In 'The Primer' in a section entitled 'The philosophy of "real"', Winnicott writes:

Eventually, after a capacity for relationships has been established, such babies can take the next step towards recognition of the essential aloneness of the human being. Eventually such a baby grows up to say 'I know that there is no direct contact between external reality and myself, only an illusion of contact, a midway phenomenon that works very well for me when I am not tired.

I couldn't care less that there is a philosophical problem involved.'
(HN114–5)

Through the mother's organization of early life, we are endowed with a sense of confidence even when faced with situations that should drive us all crazy. As I mentioned above, a crucial aspect of the maternal task is her provision of a holding environment that sustains the infant's continuity of being.

When interviewing mothers and infants, Winnicott would sit at the edge of a table and the baby would be on the mother's lap. On the table between them there would be a spatula[1], usually in a bowl. By placing this object between the baby and himself, he could discover a great deal. While the mother talked to Winnicott, the baby would look at the bowl, then at Winnicott, and back to the bowl, and up at the mother. There were many important phenomena there for observation, and by watching the baby's relation to this new object, Winnicott could assess the infant's health. He could observe the mother's relation to the baby, the mother's relation to Winnicott, the baby's relation to the mother, the baby's relation to Winnicott. In particular, he would be able to note the infant's capacity for 'object usage'.

Let us think about the difference between good enough mothering and not good enough mothering. Let us imagine that this is the object in the infant's field. *[Bollas places a pen on the lecture table.]* The infant notes this object. Mama is over here, somewhat removed. At this moment, all we are dealing with is the infant's perception of the presence of an object. But then he looks away, his mouth slackens open, he relaxes and turns back to look at the object. Now he is ready for an *experience* of the object. His mouth is ready, he is drooling; the erogenic zone is organized, and the object has become an object of desire. We can now say that he has developed an instinctual relationship to its presence.

---

[1] A tongue depressor.

The good enough mother senses the relationship between the object and the infant's perception of it and his instinctual preparation for its use. This scene is important because she notices and supports the baby's relation to reality. If the object that the baby is looking at is too far away, it cannot be ready for the mouth. So she moves it into the area of the baby's grasp. This is called 'facilitation'. She is enabling him to go from perception, to instinctual urge, to object usage and gratification—putting it in the mouth, exploring it with his tongue, and enjoying having this experience.

Grabbing the object and putting it in the mouth demonstrates Winnicott's idea of the function of aliveness sponsored by aggression. Motility organizes a need into a psychosomatic experience. After the infant puts the object in the mouth, we can say there is an integration of perception, instinct, aggression, and optical orientation, the sum of which constitutes an emotional experience that links psyche-soma with object usage.

After this wonderful experience of reality, the baby can lose interest in the object and throw it away. This is destruction. Good destruction. Such destruction of the object is crucial to the later capability for repression.

Now for not good enough mothering. By this I do not mean something that is evil or monstrous. A not good enough mother may be a very nice person who is simply too neat and tidy. She polishes the furniture and makes sure everything is spotlessly clean. She sees the baby looking at an object on the table, drooling as he gets ready to put it in his mouth. This mother responds by removing it from the table and wiping away the baby's drool, saying, 'No, no, no!' The baby will now experience a form of despair. This is not an experience of integration in relation to the object: perception, instinct, motility, aggression, and object usage do not happen. So the baby can have only an imaginary relationship to the object. From Winnicott's point of view, this is the basis of schizoid life.

Winnicott's fundamental contribution to psychoanalysis is to preserve in our minds the psychic value of the individual's experience of the parents. Experience as an integrated activity is not simply the experience of intrapsychic life, or the experience of a phenomenon that is stored in memory. It is essential to the development of the person.

This completion of experience is maintained by the ego-support provided by maternal care. The mother's active presence ensures that the infant does not have to take responsibility for his own action or feeling. At this early stage, the fundamental characteristics of the infant's ego states are primary process, primary identification, autoerotism, and primary narcissism. During the period of holding and facilitating, there is a changeover in the baby's ego state from unintegration to integration. It is at this point that the word 'disintegration' acquires meaning.

Transition from the period of holding to 'living with' occurs when the mother presents the baby with reality. Winnicott writes: 'the whole procedure of infant-care has as its main characteristic a steady presentation of the world to the infant'[2] (MP87). But such an act of management by the mother cannot be the result of deliberate, systematic thought. It must reflect 'continuous management by a human being who is consistently herself' (MP87).

In some respects, the quality of 'living with' rests upon the aliveness of the mother, who senses her infant through her own very private self. 'The mother knows she must keep alive', writes Winnicott, 'and allow the baby to feel and hear her aliveness'[3] (MP71). One way in which this may find expression is in her participatory presence in the infant's fusions of aggression and sexuality. For example, she might match her infant's oral sadism with her 'wish

[2] "From dependence towards independence in the development of the individual" (1963) in *The Maturational Process and the Facilitating Environment*(MP). London, Hogarth, 1972. pp. 83–92.
[3] 'The development of the capacity for concern' (1963) in MP, pp. 73–82.

to be imaginatively eaten'[4] (MP127). She takes pleasure in his aggressions and sexuality, echoing his own experience of instinctual gratifications. Or she provides holding that allows the infant to experience the full course of an experience, enabling love and hate to become integrated: a joining crucial to creative potential. Winnicott's very particular contribution to our understanding of this period of an infant's life was to stress the need for the full completion of an experience, as for him, infantile experiencing of love and hate in the object relationship is crucial to the infant's eventual integration of these two forces.

Experience pertains to the evolution of the self, while thinking suggests the work of psyche and mind. Before considering further his emphasis on experiencing, it is well to point out that two different mothers exist during the 'holding' and 'living with' phases.

In the earliest period of infancy, during which holding is so crucial, the infant experiences the 'environment mother'. This is the mother who 'receives all that can be called affection and sensuous co-existence'[5] (DD103) as she wards off the unpredictable and provides that management essential to the infant's well-being. The infant's self state in relation to the environment mother is that of *being*, and elsewhere Winnicott links this with a pure female element.

The phase of 'living with' involves object relationships, and this requires the infant's recognition of the 'object mother', the mother as a being in her own right. This is the mother who is the object of the id, who 'becomes the target for excited experience backed by crude instinct-tension' (DD103). The infant's state of self in relation to the object mother is that of *doing*, and Winnicott links this with the pure masculine element.

---

[4] "Classification" is there a psycho-analytic contribution to psychiatric classification" (1959–1964) in MP, pp. 124–139.
[5] "The development of the capacity for concern" in *Deprivation and Delinquency* (DD). London, Tavistock, 1984. pp. 100–105.

Gradually, through a combination of cumulative experiencing, neurobiological development, and the mother's skill in providing the infant with the right dose of both mothers, there is a fusion of these two objects. As the infant has the full course of an instinctual experience in relation to the object mother, he simultaneously has and knows the 'more quiet relationship of the baby to the environment-mother' (DD103).

For Winnicott, this split in the object world is a natural feature of object need and hence of object relating. The infant needs the environment mother for rest, holding, and going on being, but he also needs the exciting object mother as the target of instinctual aims, ruthless usage, and thoughtless dismissal. This use of the two mothers depends, of course, on the mother's management of the total situation:

> [T]he favourable circumstances necessary at this stage are these: that the mother should continue to be alive and available, available physically and available in the sense of not being preoccupied with something else. The object-mother has to be found to survive the instinct-driven episodes, which have now acquired the full force of fantasies of oral sadism and other results of fusion. Also, the environment-mother has a special function, which is to continue to be herself, to be empathic towards her infant, to be there to receive the spontaneous gesture, and to be pleased. (DD103)

From this we can see that the idea of splitting the object into good and bad does not quite apply here. It is more a matter of splitting the object into two very different good objects: the one that holds in a sensual way, the other that provides excited gratifications. It is not only the infant's urges that keep these two objects going; the good enough mother also enjoys this double function, and she communicates her pleasure in being both the environment and the object.

For Winnicott the infant's ego is not yet integrated, and it is the mother, through her care, who will make up for this ego weakness. By 'unintegration' he does not mean that the infant is not possessed of ego actions, or indeed of ego integrations. Indeed, according to Winnicott, even in the womb the foetus performs acts of ego-work that are integrative. He maintains that the foetus is already using aggression to create his own experiences.

But individual ego integrations do not in themselves add up to ego integration as a whole, which arrives only once the infant is capable of continuous differentiation of his internal world from external reality, and thus of his world from the mother's world.

During the holding phase the infant 'attains unit status', i.e. he becomes a person, an individual in his own right. Through the mother's reliable presentation of herself to the infant, he continues to experience a continuity in being, which is the basis for ego synthesis and integration. Winnicott writes that 'psychosomatic existence . . . begins to take on a personal pattern'[6] (MP 44), described as 'the psyche indwelling in the soma' (MP 45). For Winnicott, the psyche is originally 'the imaginative elaboration of . . . physical aliveness'[7] (TP244). Over time, this imaginative elaboration achieves its own pattern and is the basis for what analysts term the 'internal world'.

During the holding phase the infant develops 'a limiting membrane' (MP45) for the differentiation of me and not me. This is an ego accomplishment, not a cognitive skill. So, for example, borderline patients have the normal neurologically derived capacity to differentiate self from object, but within the context of human object relationships this will break down, and 'me' and 'not me' distinctions will be abandoned.

---

[6] 'The theory of the parent-infant relationship' (1960) in MP, pp. 37–55.
[7] "Mind and its relation to the psyche-soma" (1949) in *Through Paediatrics to Psycho-Analysis* (TP). London, Hogarth, 1975. pp. 243–254.

In infancy, as an offshoot of ego integration, there is a fusion of the 'two roots of impulsive behaviour' (MP45): sexuality and aggression. As the diffuse elements of muscle movement and muscle erotism become 'fused with the orgiastic functioning of the erotogenic zones' (MP45), aggression is integrated with the erotic. This fusion is entirely dependent on good enough maternal care during the holding environment.

Since the physical holding of the infant is a form of loving, perhaps we could argue that the fusion of aggression and sexuality is that phenomenon that leads to sensuality. Here, at least, we could define this as a subject's pleasure in his own body-self being, derived from the mother's pleasure in holding him. Sensuality then is less a narcissistic representation than it is the subject of the simultaneous expression of the mother's pleasure in handling his body, and his own pleasure in fusing aggression and sexuality through the mother's hands.

Winnicott emphasizes how during the holding phase the infant is absolutely dependent on the mother. However, this involves a paradox: it does not mean that the infant is incapable of independent actions, but he is dependent upon the mother's care to sustain these. In this way, independent actions are themselves entirely dependent.

At the same time, however, the infant is not dependent on the mother for the nature of his personality. The ultimate source of independence in all of us, our inherited potential, is there in us from the beginning. 'We can say that the facilitating environment makes possible the steady progress of the maturational process. But the environment does not make the child. At best it enables the child to realize potential'[8] (MP85).

Those who mistakenly think of Winnicott as an environmentalist would do well to read this passage again. The environment

---

[8] "From dependence towards independence in the development of the individual" (1963) in *The Maturational Process and the Facilitating Environment* pp83–92

is crucial only as the basis for supporting the infant's realization of his personality potential. The parents are in fact 'dependent on the infant's inherited tendencies' (MP85). While other analytic theorists might provide the reader with an array of technical terms with which to itemize the infant's evolution in these first years of life, Winnicott has a particular way of sketching the stages of dependence to independence, as if in describing this evolution he shares the relativity of it. In opting for the description of principles or attitudes, he offers a 'kind of blueprint for existentialism' (MP86). He maintains that the initial stage of absolute dependence on the mother is followed by a stage of relative dependence, in which 'one can distinguish between dependence that is quite beyond the infant's ken, and dependence that the infant can know about' (MP87). In the stage of relative dependence the infant uses the mother's progressive failures of adaptation to his own benefit.

3

True Self

In conceiving the term 'true self', Winnicott did so reluctantly. He regarded it as necessary in order to discuss the 'false self'. Its original status was as a supply term, to stand in for the opposite of that anxiety state that generated the false self.

One can find its earliest formulation in the 1941 paper 'The observation of infants in a set situation', when Winnicott describes the infant's 'free bodily movement' in the use of an object (TP54). This free movement of the infant in his body, he will later state, is an important feature of the true self. Then in 1952, in 'Anxiety associated with insecurity', he wrote of the infant's 'centre of gravity of consciousness' which is the 'kernel to the shell' (TP99). Here he locates this kernel within the total unit of mother and baby; a view he will slightly alter later with the formulation of the concept of the true self:

> Before object relationships the state of affairs is this: that the unit is not the individual, the unit is an environment-individual set-up. The centre of gravity of the being does not start off in the individual. It is in the total set-up. (TP99)

Later (1960),[1] Winnicott will write that the true self, which arises out of the inherited potential, requires maternal care in order to come to life: 'the True Self does not become a living reality except as a result of the mother's repeated success in meeting the infant's spontaneous gesture or sensory hallucination' (MP145).

[1] See 'Ego distortion in terms of true and false self' (1960) in MP, pp. 140–152.

Essential Aloneness. Christopher Bollas, Oxford University Press. © Christopher Bollas 2024.
DOI: 10.1093/oso/9780197683880.003.0003

As the mother meets the infant's spontaneous gesture, she makes it real and develops the infant's capacity to use gesture as embodied signifier. This is the foundation of future infant symbolizations. It is also an intermediate stage in the child's eventual use of language. It is of interest that in work with autistic children who do not speak, some therapists will aim to go back to the essentials of responding to the child's gestures, by playing with the child and by working with the mother to help her to do this. Such therapy implicitly recognizes the gestural foundations of symbols and language.

In a sense, the true self *is* aliveness. It is not reactive to the environment but is primary: 'it comes from the aliveness of the body tissues and the working of body-functions, including the heart's action and breathing' (MP148). Partly for this reason, Winnicott saw the true self as a form of the Id, as 'little more than the summation of sensori-motor aliveness' (MP149).

In fact, I think it is much more than that, and I take my cue from Winnicott's important statement that the true self is the inherited 'personality potential'. From my point of view, this is exactly what it is: a complex inherited core of personality present at birth, an idiom of being and relating that will evolve and become activated according to the infant's experience of the mother.

Let us review Winnicott's theory of the self.

He argues that some element of self is present in the state of aloneness that we carry with us through life. Aloneness precedes aliveness, which in turn comes before dependency and instinct. It is characterized fundamentally by continuity in being, and this is contingent upon a sufficient absence of interruptions of existence. The self begins with the inherited disposition, the ancestral history of the self encoded in DNA, the 'kernel' of one's being. This true self has potential. In order for this to develop, it requires the facilitating empathy and work of the mother and the father. It will only become personality through experiencing; it is experiencing that allows the true self to emerge into reality.

What are the particular features of the true self? How do we know what it is? How do we see it? For Winnicott, it has to do first and foremost with what he calls 'aliveness', the quality of the person's way of being. Attending to this quality of aliveness is a central focus in Winnicottian analysis. One criticism that he makes of classical psychoanalysis is that the analyst can analyse the patient, but this will never bring the patient into creative living.

The other main quality of the true self is 'spontaneity': the gesture made real. We see somebody we would like to talk to, and we approach them and introduce ourselves. This is the gesture made real. If we merely think about doing this but we don't actually move towards the person, the gesture is accomplished only as an inner mental representation. So one of the ways to evaluate the evolution of an individual's true self is to note the extent to which their gestures have been made real.

In this example I am speaking of the relation of the individual to the external world. Winnicott also talks about the psyche as the imaginative elaboration of body existence. This is another way of talking about instincts. Instinctual life is a strong feature of true self.

We can say that the infant's body determines the early imagining, and many of his first gestures are elaborations of inner body experience. If the mother is good enough, this imaginative elaboration resonates within the object world, giving the infant a sense of inner personal reality.

This is a quite difficult concept, because 'inner personal reality' is not the same thing as 'internal world'. Our internal world will be populated by many object representations, some of which may sponsor anxiety. Inner personal reality has more to do, I think, with a sense that our own internal state is sufficiently in rapport with the environment to allow us to feel that we are the author of our own existence.

In some ways, inner personal reality refers to the quality of subjectivity. We all know there are some patients who provide a clear and elaborate narrative of their lives, but it is as if they are talking about another person. They are not conveying the fundamentals of a 'me' that is organized for experiencing. This is why for Winnicottian analysts it is not enough simply to analyse the content of the patient's narrative; they need to find some way to address the basic split in the personality.

Ultimately, Winnicott's theory of aliveness and expressed spontaneity implies a theory of sensuality and pleasure. This, in my view, is one of the gaps in psychoanalytic theory. Sensuality is different from sexuality. Sensuality has something to do with psychosomatic integration and positive narcissism; with pleasure in being oneself. Do we really think that the accomplishment of genital primacy is the final evolution of the libido? I don't think we can be satisfied with this, and it is equally impossible to create a simple ideal of sensuality.

We can also distinguish between instinct (or impulse) and pleasure. Here is another gap in our theory: we don't talk enough about pleasure. How do we analyse the patient's pleasure in being with the analyst? How do we notice it? How do we make room for it? Sometimes I think we prefer to focus on instinct or impulses because it protects us from having to talk about pleasure. If I enjoy a patient, if I take pleasure in their presence, are the two of us being patient and analyst together? Is this to be forbidden, exiled from psychoanalytic discourse?

Of course we know that we should not gratify the patient. However, there is a difference between gratification of experiences, and recognition and understanding of gratification that *already exists in object relating*. We need to consider how to convey in an appropriate way our understanding of the patient's pleasure in our existence and his gratification at being with us. This needs to be made a part of the total field of psychoanalysis.

In other words, Winnicott discusses elements of psychoanalysis that we have neglected, that we have allowed to escape our attention. The story of psychoanalysis, from its beginnings to the present day is, in part, the history of movements of people who have suffered persecutions. It is understandable, therefore, that the focus in psychoanalysis has been on destruction, on loss, grief, and mourning. But I believe that we must now try to re-find what Freud was writing about, in various ways, before the First World War. This has to do with the nature of sexuality, the history of libido, and the establishment of desire.

4

Becoming a Living Reality

It is worth reminding ourselves of the important function of the mother in integrating her infant. If she 'meets . . . infantile omnipotence revealed in a gesture (or a sensori-motor grouping)' (MP145), she links the infant's movements to external reality. Such continuous, repeated linking of his inner needs and wishes to the actual object world supports the logic of true self existence and the maturational process.

The child possesses a conviction that he can bring his own idiom of person to bear upon external objects in order to receive pleasure and gratification. But the mother also derives pleasure from being used, or made use of, by the child. Both as a child and in later life, a person who lives from the true self will enjoy the double satisfactions of receiving pleasure and of giving pleasure. Gratifications in interpersonal relations are simultaneously pleasurable for self and other.

Think of two people who are at dinner or in conversation, swapping stories and observations, enjoying one another in a way that is mutually useful and mentally pleasurable. In this example each makes use of the other to play—but we should also consider the pleasures of argumentation. An intellectual disagreement allows for pleasurable aggression as each participant 'destroys' the other's position only to find that the other survives the destruction and counters with another good point. Such inter-aggressivity is not unlike some dialectics between infant and mother. When true self is free to be at play, self and other experience a pleasing, almost sensory mixture of aggression, intellect, somatic alertness, gestural aliveness, and enjoyment in being together.

Essential Aloneness. Christopher Bollas, Oxford University Press. © Christopher Bollas 2024.
DOI: 10.1093/oso/9780197683880.003.0004

Guilt over victories may ensue but, if so, reparations derived from mutual pleasure are not difficult to achieve so long as the atmosphere is receptive to reparation. Often, both participants will have had moments of being victorious, the field of difference strewn with the traces of rhetoric conquests and defeats. The pleasures of interrelating obviate the experience of guilt and the need for reparation.

The true self becomes 'a living reality ... as a result of the mother's repeated success in meeting the infant's spontaneous gesture or sensory hallucination' (MP145). For Winnicott, this link between the infant's gesture and the mother's action is the foundation of the symbolic, a theory of symbolism that emerges out of intersubjective creativity. Eventually the child comes to use and interpret the symbolic as he discovers his inner feelings through the gestures he makes and the mother's interpretation of them. So, in an important sense, the mother creates the infant's reality by linking his inner state to the actual world, i.e. to herself. Winnicott writes: 'It is the infant's *gesture or hallucination* that is made real, and the capacity of the infant *to use a symbol* is the result' (MP145). If, however, the mother does the opposite, if she imposes her own set of expectations and demands upon the infant at too early a stage, then he will substitute her needs for his.

Infant and mother participate in a mediated reality. No mother continuously adapts to her infant. In fact, Winnicott suggests that all good enough mothers mess up, and that children benefit from such failure. They use such experience to collect together a tolerance for subsequent frustrations and to establish a differentiated sense of the limits of an object's offerings. As the infant matures and the mother decreases her adaptation, she provides graduated disillusion. Increasingly, she will actively refuse the infant's gesture in order to substitute it with her own demands and those of the wider world.

Does this foster false self compliance in the infant? It might do, if it were a characteristic of this mother that she imposed on her baby too soon. But it might also be to the continued benefit of the infant if she conveys her demand with her own pleasurable aggression. It is not the establishment of the demands in itself, but the emotional attitude behind the maternal act that will or will not move the infant into the compliance that sponsors a false self.

Winnicott writes that if the mother's adaptation is good enough, the infant comes to believe in reality. So cathexis of the object depends on maternal solicitation of the infant's psychic economy. She invites him into interrelating.

5

False Self

Winnicott's terminology changes through the different phases of his life. In the 1940s and the early 1950s, he frequently writes about 'psyche' and 'psyche-soma', and he uses 'psyche' more frequently than 'ego'. In the 1950s and 1960s he uses the terms 'true self' and 'false self', and in the 1960s 'ego' appears more frequently than 'psyche'. I am going to try here to integrate these various theories in order to clarify the concept of the false self.

He writes that the basis of psyche is soma. Soma comes first, and psyche emerges as the imaginative elaboration of physical functions, somatic parts and feelings. It concerns physical aliveness, or aliveness imagined.

Early functions of psyche concern the binding together of past experiences, potentialities, and the present moment. It involves awareness and the binding of an expectancy for the future. As a result of this, the 'bound' self comes into existence. Mind, which he distinguishes from psyche, begins (and this is Winnicott's poetry) as 'a flourish on the edge of psycho-somatic functioning' (HN26).

He says that, in the beginning, mind evolves as that part of psyche-soma that is concerned with environmental failure. The mind has its roots in the need of the individual to have a perfect environment. If the mind has to deal with too many erratic environmental experiences, this disturbs continuity of being, and there is a need to organize the environment. The mind then becomes at odds with the psyche-soma, which it tries to take over. The following passage is from Winnicott's paper 'Mind and its Relation to the Psyche-Soma' (1946):

Essential Aloneness. Christopher Bollas, Oxford University Press. © Christopher Bollas 2024.
DOI: 10.1093/oso/9780197683880.003.0005

Certain kinds of failure on the part of the mother, especially erratic behaviour, produce over-activity of the mental functioning.
Here, in the overgrowth of the mental function reactive to erratic
mothering, we see that there can develop an opposition between
the mind and the psyche-soma, since in reaction to this abnormal
environmental state the thinking of the individual begins to take
over and organize the caring for the psyche-soma, whereas in
health it is the function of the environment to do this.[1] (TP246)

So when the environment becomes too erratic, the mind must become active. Psyche-soma then starts to depend on the mind instead of on the environment. One can see this clinically in patients
who have depended for so long on the mind that they are incapable
of using the other as an object. So when the analyst makes an interpretation, they will need to restate it or add to it, or dissect it in
order to make it their own. Winnicott writes: 'In health the mind
does not usurp the environment's function, but makes possible an
understanding and eventually a making use of its relative failure'
(TP246).

In the extreme . . . in the earliest stages we find

mental functioning becoming a thing in itself, practically replacing
the good mother and making her unnecessary. Clinically, this can
go along with dependence on the actual mother and a false personal growth on a compliance basis. This is a most uncomfortable
state of affairs, especially because the psyche of the individual
gets 'seduced' away into this mind from the intimate relationship
which the psyche originally had with the soma. The result is a
mind-psyche, which is pathological. (TP246-7)

The important point here is that mind replaces mother.

---

[1] 'Mind and its relation to the psyche-soma' (1949) in TP, pp. 243-254.

Psyche becomes absorbed in mental functioning, and there is then a split between psyche and soma. Winnicott says the intellect cannot be ill, only the psyche can. Psyche is that part of the individual concerned with relationship to the body and to the external world. It becomes a thing with a capacity to create and to perceive external reality.

This idea is very difficult. Winnicott is trying to conceptualize the origin of what is distinctively human in our way of being, thinking, and experiencing.

In my terms, psyche registers the idiom of a person. I mention this now because Winnicott makes a further specification of his theory of mind. Because mind is concerned with impingements, or the disruption of continuity of being, it is influenced by factors not specifically personal to the individual.

If impingements are excessive and they continually create intense reactions on the part of the mind, this cannot be encompassed by psyche; it can only be catalogued. This type of mind becomes a burden for psyche-soma; it acts like a foreign body, as if it is beyond understanding. Winnicott sometimes makes a reference to obsessional neurosis as an example of this experience of mind on the part of psyche-soma.

He then proceeds to talk about how mind is given a localization. We locate mind in the head because we cannot see our head, just as we cannot see our mind. Later he talks about the error of the neurosurgeon who believes that by cutting away part of the brain he can remove part of the mind. One of the aims of psychosomatic illness, he says, is to draw the psyche away from the mind, back to its original intimate association with soma. This is what he means by the positive side of illness.

This brings us to Winnicott's classification of the false self, which he outlined in his 1960 essay 'Ego distortion in terms of true and false self'.[2] This emerges out of his theory of the mind as the object

---

[2] In MP, pp. 140–152.

that replaces the environment—the original object of dependence and of cathexis. He describes five classifications of false self. In the first case, what he describes as being 'at one extreme':

> [T]he False Self sets up as real and it is this that observers tend to think is the real person. In living relationships, work relationships, and friendships, however, the False Self begins to fail. In situations in which what is expected is a whole person, the False Self has some essential lacking. At this extreme the True Self is hidden. (MP142–3)

This is the patient for whom mental functioning has become the sole means through which they negotiate all of their cathexis, all of their relations. It has become their technique of adaptation. When they come into analysis, however, they encounter an environment, created by the psychoanalyst, which in some respects has nothing for the patient in terms of a solitary use of mind. The patient's efforts to negotiate his way through the analysis by maintaining his dependence on mind does not work effectively because the environment does not require this type of object relationship. We see how the obsessional patient demonstrates the functions of mind in our presence, as if we are not there. Or how the narcissistic patient exhibits the mind in order to elicit our admiration of and dependence upon mind. Winnicott often refers to intelligent, gifted patients who in the early part of the analysis cease having anything to say from the mind. They are then truly at a loss; they lose any sense of who they are or what they are truly thinking.

Describing the second type, he writes:

> The False Self defends the True Self; the True Self is, however, acknowledged as a potential and is allowed a secret life. Here is the clearest example of clinical illness as an organization with a positive aim, the preservation of the individual in spite of abnormal

environmental conditions. This is an extension of the psycho-analytic concept of the value of symptoms to the sick person. (MP143)

The third category, 'more towards health':

> The False Self has as its main concern a search for the conditions which make it possible for the True Self to come into its own. (MP143)

The fourth category, 'still further towards health' is the world of the 'imaginary' as Lacan would formulate it. Winnicott maintains that the fourth category is 'built on identifications' (MP143), which implicitly recognizes the value of relations in the eventual facilitation of the true self.

The fifth category, 'in health':

> [T]he False Self is represented by the whole organization of the polite and mannered social attitude, a 'not wearing the heart on the sleeve', as might be said. Much has gone to the individual's ability to forgo omnipotence and the primary process in general, the gain being the place in society which can never be attained or maintained by the True Self alone. (MP143)

Of course it is not possible for the true self to live an unmedi-ated existence in a social space. Ordinary false self is essential to the aliveness of the human being, to the preservation of ordinary privacy, and to the guarantee that one's internal world remains internal.

What I think we have not written enough about is the person for whom the problem is not representations of the false self but a pre-mature and dangerous expression of true self. A person living from the false self is concerned with compliance, with adaptation, and the nature of his life is one of reacting rather than of a continuity of being. These are the patients who wait for us to speak so they can react to our comments, or who bring endless stories of their reactions to events in their lives. Because this is more or less all they can do. They do not know how to initiate experience, so they have developed a reactive way of living.

6

On Celebration and Ruthlessness

As we know, it is the facilitating capability of the mother that makes true self evolution possible. For an infant, one of the main features of this will be her capacity to hold and integrate the baby. The evolution of true self depends upon the containing function of the mother.

Eventually the infant internalizes her containing process. In a good enough situation, the infant develops an assumption about the usefulness of mind because of the reliability of the mind of the mother. However, if the child experiences the containing element of the mother as destructive, then mind may become something that could be very frightening. The child can then develop an intellectual inhibition and may attack thinking as a way of demonstrating the experience of the maternal mind.

In this sort of case, the analyst's understanding of the child's symbolic representations shows the child the usefulness of mind. Although interpretations of the symbolic representations may not be made use of by the child in an obvious and specific way, the analyst's thinking demonstrates the trustworthiness of mind. In other words, the child learns to trust the containing mental function of the analyst.

If there has been a failure in the development of true self, what is its fate? Winnicott always thinks of it as something that is secret, or that has been withheld. He does not talk about it in terms of fragmentation or as creating a split location.

Of course, it must be possible for the child's psyche to project true self potential into another object, so elements of an individual's true self are projected into the object world and kept there for a time.

Essential Aloneness. Christopher Bollas, Oxford University Press. © Christopher Bollas 2023.
DOI: 10.1093/oso/9780197683880.003.0006

Such projection would not be of a fundamentally persecutory kind; it would represent the preservation of a possibility. For example, I saw a patient, a psychotic-hysteric, who had many photographs of a famous celebrity. This person became a projection of her true self. In her case, projective identification conveyed and stored true self potential.

In the psychoanalytical relationship, a patient may maintain projective identifications of true self until she experiences the mind of the analyst as safe enough, or good enough, to think and to metabolize her own true self. In other words, if true self is given the right kind of experience in object relating, this facilitates what Winnicott terms *personalization*. Personalization has to do with the evolution of true self into creative living. We are not talking about the qualitative factor of individual life, or the internal world per se, but about the self's experience of the object, which gives rise to a confident belief that relating can be nourishing. We become a person through relationship. This is a crucial point for Winnicott.

One alternative would be the schizoid solution, in which richness exists but only in the internal world. This is a situation in which the child does not develop the use of the living world in a way that feels creative. A schizoid person might write a great novel or a symphony as an alternative to creativity in living. And children who are very gifted can sometimes turn exclusively to the internal world as a means of trying to realize elements of true self. As Winnicott says, for the schizoid, mind becomes the alternative to the other.

Clinically, especially when working with children, it is interesting to consider how we analyse and work with the true self, and analyse the false self. From the Winnicottian perspective, analysis of defence, or anxiety, or persecutory states is analysis of the false self. This will always involve analysing at least three people: child, mother, and father—and often also family.

Where is true self during sustained analysis of the false self? I think at times it has its existence in the imaginative, aggressive, and spirited existence of the analyst's countertransference. At some point the patient understands that it is a question of whether the analyst is going to survive and live creatively, or whether he is going to 'die'. The analyst's dying will be represented by his clinical failure. Interpretive work is, generally speaking, a function of the analyst's creativity: it involves the expression of true self in the clinical situation. Fortunately, most patients identify with the analyst's deliberate, aggressive, lively, interpretive confrontation with the false self. But there are some people whose hatred of true self has become so intense they must destroy the true self of the analyst, thereby destroying the analysis.

How does this happen? There are patients whose persecuting challenge in the transference creates a false self in the analyst. I am thinking here of how the hysteric forces us to make use of psychoanalytic techniques as false self. Our inner creativity is made problematic, and we find ourselves withdrawing from a spontaneous interplay into a quieter, more withdrawn, interpretive relation to this crazy person.

I believe that the false self in the patient can be analysed. However, I do not think that it is possible, nor would it be desirable, to analyse the true self. It can only be celebrated. And this is where I get into trouble with some of my psychoanalytical colleagues, who suggest that I am gratifying the patient or that I am abandoning analysis. I do not believe that I am doing this. I think it is very important at certain moments to support and celebrate the patient's view of the analyst and of the analytical situation as an object.

Let me give an example. In working with Alex, a manic-depressive patient, I was immediately struck by his extraordinary presentation. He was a very big man, and he always wore black clothing. He was very grandiose, occasionally threatening, and he had fantasies of being the Messiah. At the beginning, I wondered whether I could endure the analysis.

But fortunately Alex was very depressed for the first months, so I had space to say what I thought before a manic period arrived. A tradition emerged between us concerning the analysis of his manic system and false identifications. When he became manic, and the sessions were verbally violent, I would interrupt him with the words, 'I want to say what I think.'

Of course, he was very irritated by this. He was delivering a great oration, and this was a privileged moment. I was interrupting his account of his preparation for the salvation of mankind with my own impoverished language—insulting him, moreover, by suggesting that his great ideas were a reflection of his own despair and impotence. He found these interruptions infuriating, and he would tell me in no uncertain terms to be quiet. I told him that I wasn't going to be quiet. At one moment he said that he could kill me. I said, 'Why? That would be redundant—you already are killing me.'

For many months, session after session would be characterized by his violent fury with me for interpreting to him what he was saying. I did not do what ego psychology and others recommended at the time: I did not support his defences. Instead, I persisted in analysing his manic structure and his grandiose delusions.

I did this in a particular kind of way. I would say, 'Alex, you're not going to like what I'm thinking.' Or, 'Well, you've been very angry with me, and now you are really going to hate me.' I would then make my interpretation, and he would say, 'Christ no!' or, 'I already know what you think. Why don't you shut up!' I would wait and then reply, 'I know you want me to shut up, but I'm going to tell you what I think.'

It went on like this for a long time. After a while, when Alex came into sessions I sensed that he was beginning to enjoy our confrontations, taking pleasure in our verbal combat. The character of his personality was becoming less manic and more aggressive. Whereas at first I was not even in his thoughts—he was addressing the world—now he started to make fun of me, and I would celebrate his brilliant mockery. He could be very critical in a wonderfully eventful manner, and I would laugh and say, 'Extraordinarily well said!' I wanted to celebrate the positive side of the manic illness, the creative side.

Making fun of me constituted affectionate aggression. He was relating to me, and I wanted to support and celebrate the development of object relationship. For Alex, the discovery that he could bring true aggression to his relation to the other, and enjoy the situation, was a major accomplishment.

Winnicott believed that the infant's ego is in a state of unintegration. The concept of unintegration does not depend on cognitive ability. It has to do with the coming together of the different parts of the self, and it is therefore an accomplishment of psyche, not the mind.

We can say that if the mother and the baby cannot find a good enough relationship, then the infant's true self does not materialize into object relating, and at this point psychological illness becomes inevitable. Winnicott points out that when the infant complies with the object world from a very early stage, perhaps by being particularly sweet and charming, we can see the evolution of false self in the first months of life.

One of the essential features of health in the baby is the capacity for ruthlessness in the use of the object. In relating to the mother, when he is feeding at the breast, he needs to be able to not think of her but to eat her up, destroy her and then find her again. It is important to see how Winnicott differs with Melanie Klein's theory of destruction with this crucial concept of positive destructiveness.

The concept of positive destructiveness is almost straight out of Hegel's *Phenomenology of Spirit*. Ruthless use of the object is what Winnicott means by primary love. And we can see that aggression and libido (instinctual desire) come together and become fused in this moment. If ruthlessness is not accomplished, or if the infant's ruthless use of the object is disturbed, then we can see the breeding ground of mental illness.

No doubt because he was a paediatrician, Winnicott noticed the hypochondriac and psychosomatic punctuations of early infant despair. So, for example, he would see a baby who had difficulties with swallowing, or would vomit, or had problems with defecation.

Winnicott knew that these somatic operations of taking in and eliminating might also be metaphorical acts expressing states of mind. The baby who cannot feed may be saying, 'I can't take this in.' A child who cannot defecate may be saying, 'I cannot get rid of what I take in.' A baby who is always defecating or urinating indiscriminately, without a sense of boundary, may be saying, 'I cannot hold anything in for long.'

In other words, he was seeing many ways in which infants demonstrate psychological problems through somatic states. And of course he was noticing the nature of the mother's relationship to the baby, and it was this relationship that he was aiming to cure. For example, in talking about the infant's development of the 'capacity for concern', he emphasizes that the infant's aggressive and destructive potential is often greater than his reparative ability. So when the infant destroys the mother in his mind, he feels that there is little he can do to sufficiently make up for the destruction.

As adults, we have many ways to be reparative if we have been destructive. We can apologize, buy flowers. We can make reparation. But where does the infant's reparative capacity come from?

When he addresses the problem of the depressive position in this period of development, we can see how Winnicott focuses on the contribution of the mother. He says that one smile from the mother's face is equivalent to an entire day's work of infantile reparation.

It is important to understand that the mother conveys to her infant her pleasure in what is intrinsically human. At first the infant cannot project humanity into the object, but he feels the human, sophisticated love in the mother and takes it in. In time, he learns to project it for its own purpose, but we cannot assume that the young infant already possesses the structures for projection. He needs to discover these capacities and structures from within the mother, and out of this matrix new projective capabilities emerge.

The problem in the schizophrenic baby, from Winnicott's point of view, is that the baby who is already moving into schizophrenia is mentally dying. The infant has little sense of being reflected or received or seen by the mother, so his instinctual life cannot be integrated with his cognitive development. In my view, the manic-depressive baby cannot make successful reparation to the mother because of hate. To some extent, for manic patients their sense of time is almost equivalent to the temporality of the unconscious that Freud speaks of. The messianic manic patient lives in a timeless world. Because he has been unable to bind a sense of time through object relating, there has been no reception for his reparation. And as he has been unable to save one person, he must therefore become the Messiah in order to rescue the whole of mankind.

7

Transitional Objects

Let us begin with a quote from Winnicott in his 1951 paper, 'Transitional Objects and Transitional Phenomena':

> I have introduced the terms 'transitional objects' and 'transitional phenomena' for designation of the intermediate area of experience, between the thumb and the teddy bear, between the oral erotism and true object relationship, between primary creative activity and projection of what has already been introjected, between primary unawareness of indebtedness and the acknowledgement of indebtedness, ('Say: Ta!'). (TP230)

Let us deconstruct his definition to try and get at Winnicott's core message. He writes: 'I have introduced the terms "transitional objects" and "transitional phenomena" for designation of the intermediate area of experience.' The crucial word here is 'designation'. He uses the terms as arbitrary signifiers, in order to identify an area of experience. As we shall discuss, this is an intermediate area: an in-between state. It is not specifically located either inside the psyche or in the outside world.

Unfortunately, Winnicott overburdened the notion of an intermediate area between forms of object usage by using it in a number of different ways. It can be thumb sucking, cuddling the teddy bear, or a particular type of object relating such as oral erotism and true object relationships. It can also refer to forms of mental life that exist between primary creativity and the projection of the introject. Finally, it can be used for an intermediate place between

Essential Aloneness. Christopher Bollas, Oxford University Press. © Christopher Bollas 2024.
DOI: 10.1093/oso/9780197683880.003.0007

two positions, for example unawareness of indebtedness and acknowledgement of indebtedness.

However, in his next paragraph, Winnicott's unique way of speaking gives the cited above context. He writes:

> By this definition an infant's babbling or the way an older child goes over a repertoire of songs and tunes while preparing for sleep come within the intermediate area as transitional phenomena, along with the use made of objects that are not part of the infant's body yet and are not fully recognized as belonging to external reality. (TP230)

The important point here is that a process, in this case the infant's babbling, is a transitional phenomenon that takes place within the intermediate area. It is the intermediate quality of the space that constitutes the phenomenon that Winnicott is describing. Objects may come into this space, but they are not in themselves the essence of the intermediate.

It is important to emphasize this because much that has been written on transitional objects implies that it is the object in and of itself that defines transitionality. For example, an infant might be playing with a piece of fluff. Does this necessarily constitute a transitional object? No, it does not. In order for an object to be transitional, it must be utilized within a particular area of experience, within the intermediate area that exists between the strictly internal, the area of hallucination and pure wish, and the strictly external, the area of the actual object world.

In this paper Winnicott proceeds to clarify his concept further. He says that our customary psychoanalytic understanding of human nature—fundamentally an inner reality that can be rich or poor—is not sufficient. Between the inner and the outer worlds, there exists 'a third part of the life of a human being, a part that we cannot ignore, an intermediate area of *experiencing*, to which inner reality and external life both contribute' (TP230).

The crucial word here is 'experiencing'.

Although Winnicott was not endeavouring to make a profound philosophical point, it is as if he is taking Hegel's reply to Kant's *Critique of Pure Reason* in his *Phenomenology of Spirit* and saying yes, it is true that we do not grasp the thing in itself, but we have an *experience* of the thing in itself. Although we cannot represent this thing, we have experienced it and have been shaped by it.

One of the most important features of Winnicottian clinical technique is the analyst's effort to identify and to support true self activity in sessions. The development of transference and the use of the analyst as a transference object are not equivalent to the emergence of true self. This arrives through a certain type of liveliness and uninhibited thoughtfulness.

Pleasure in difference comes in many ways, but it is possible to develop it only if the analyst is willing to create a space in which this can take place. Winnicott's attention—and this was true also of Masud Khan, Marion Milner, and other Independents—would focus on the patient's capacity (or incapacity) to be alive in the room with the analyst; alive in their sense of animation, in their aggression, in their sensuality, in their playfulness. These analysts' attention was directed as much to this aspect as it was to the transference. This space of experiencing is not allied to the inner or the outer and, although it may offer a rendezvous, it does not aim to produce a synthesis between them. In fact, it is as if the categories of inner and outer are nonexistent. This is a creative feature of ambiguity. Analytical clarity or focus in such moments would foreclose the patient's use of the intermediate space.

Patients sense that psychoanalysis is a very special form of theatre. It is a place for representations, narrations, re-experiencings. For example, let us say that a patient talks about his father in a way that is both wistful and critical. Does he believe that he is giving a true account of his father?

I doubt it. When Laertes jumps into the grave with Hamlet and we are in anguish over this terrible, bizarre confusion between them, do we actually think they are going to kill each other—that we are going to end up with two dead actors on the stage? No. But our feelings are as intense as if it were so. Equally, when the patient talks sadly about his father, do we treat it as if it is pure hallucination? I hope not. Some psychoanalysts, I'm afraid, use every opportunity they can to interpret a patient's narrative objects as references to the transference. So the patient says 'I am thinking of my father. I feel sad because I don't believe that he has ever understood me, and it makes me angry.' The analyst might say something like 'I think you feel angry with this analytic father too, and sad at the state of affairs between the two of us.' This is a transference interpretation of the here-and-now.

In fact I do believe that the most important interpretations that we make are transference interpretations in the here-and-now, but it is as if we have become so in love with our own invention that we exploit it. Some analysts make such interpretations every few minutes. Of course it makes our highly complex job rather simple, and this is alluring. But it is this sort of habitual analytic action that inspired Winnicott to write *Playing and Reality*, because he was concerned that analysts' exploitation of the patient's narrative for predetermined psychoanalytical purposes foreclosed true experiencing. If the patient who sadly criticizes his father is met automatically with a transference interpretation, this can deprive him of his quietly evolving experience of his father.

In both the Classical Freudian and the Kleinian traditions there has been a consistent and shared emphasis on the analysis of 'clinical material'. This term concretizes something immensely complex. I think of it now as a very strange way to talk about a patient's presence in analysis. On the other hand, perhaps it metaphorizes what we have done to the session. We have made it into a substance— earth to earth, ashes to ashes, dust to dust. We deaden the situation, I think, when we use the word 'material' and insist upon it for our own didactic purposes.

The patient's material is the stuff of narrative. It is what the person talks about. To simplify Winnicott, we could say that by 'experiencing' he means the nature of the person's presence within the psychoanalytical space. The Classical analyst might say that this is a well-known phenomenon, and that the Classical theory of affects addresses this issue. In the analytic space the patient might be anxious, or joyful, or depressed, or eager. This is the patient's experience in that space.

A Kleinian analyst might reply that they place great emphasis on the patient's experiencing in the session by carefully noting how he makes use of analytic interpretation, whether he integrates the analyst's words, or projects parts of himself into the analyst, or aspects of the analyst's interpretation, into a narrative object.

Do these views of experiencing—the Classical view of the patient's affective state and the Kleinian view of the patient's introjective and projective responses—address what Winnicott is talking about? In my view, the intermediate space that he identifies is not defined in either Classical or Kleinian theory. Neither tradition has a concept of a space in the analysis in which the patient's experiencing is the vector of analytic movement, or of an experiencing which is not an affect state or an intersubjective movement, but which allows for the patient's creation of meaning.

We play, and we take pleasure in the value of our existence. To experience our life is to feel the emergence of the true self through the medium of transitional space, where there is no claim for significance, either from the auditors of internal reality, the psychoanalyst, or of external reality—the sociologist or, unfortunately in some cases, the state.

For Winnicott, the true self and its facilitation evolves into a personal pattern in the course of a psychoanalysis, and transitional space is crucial to this evolution. Through this facilitation and the creation of this space, something of the core of the person establishes itself.

Is this focus different from that suggested by Freud's theory of the unconscious?

The Freudian model, which we all use and which is very important to us, centres itself more or less around the idea of repression and the return of the repressed. Therefore it has as its aim the uncovering of what has been too painful to bear and the reintegration of these painful feelings into the ego. There is an effort to analyse the source of conflict in order to release the affects associated with it.

The true self cannot be articulated within Freudian theory. It is not alive in the topographical model, as it is neither the dynamically repressed unconscious nor the primary repressed unconscious. The true self is an inherited disposition. Winnicott believes in the centrality of genetic inheritance. This is there before birth, and it forms the core of the person. The question is, how does this true self evolve within the system of maternal care? How can the analyst create conditions for the rediscovery of true self and its re-emergence?

Let us try to define the intermediate area of experience in this room. Here we all are. During this rather long discourse, many of you will have wandered off into the internal world, having fantasies and daydreams, or reminding yourself what you must do this afternoon. The intermediate area of experience is not this communing with the internal world, nor is it the text of my lecture, which for our purposes is the basis of your external reality in this room.

So where is the area of experiencing? Well, it will be present in those moments when I might say something that you find inspiring or moving, and you play with it, you take it into your mind for a while and enjoy it. And that is enough.

If I go on too long, you will become tired and no longer able to use this experience. You might then resort to writing down what I say. From a Winnicottian point of view, this would be using the mind as a defence against reality: that is, trying to make the ideas work for you by writing them down, because you are tired and can no longer think. Alternatively you might go back into daydreams and fantasies, or become delinquent and turn to your neighbour to talk about something more interesting.

Of course, in a room this large and with so many people, it is not right to generalize about a transitional space or intermediate experiencing. But if I were to speak in a dull, monotonous way so that you found my voice unbearable, or if everything I said was predictable, then your use of me would not take place. That is, you would not be able to use me to elaborate your own inner creativity. There would be no experiencing of me. This is what Winnicott is trying to talk about when describing the analytical situation.

So what is the task of the analyst? It is to create a space where it is possible for the patient to use the analyst. If I pointed at someone here in the audience and said, 'Now would you please tell me what I have been talking about for the last forty-five minutes?' do we think this person would be capable at that moment of living inside a transitional space? No. His anxiety would be so high that there would be no question of this being possible.

In Classical psychoanalysis the patient is under an obligation to report what he is thinking to the analyst. This is called 'the work of an analysis'. Silence is treated as a resistance which must be overcome. In my view, a person who has this inner obligation will be incapable of the kind of experiencing that we have been talking about this morning.

How can we define the gratification of the true self's experiencing of its unfolding? Is it an instinctual pleasure? It involves the body, but it is not the body of instinctual function. It is perhaps more to the point to say that this is the pleasure of the body ego, or the pleasure of coming into being, the ego's desire.

In his paper 'The capacity to be alone' (1958),[1] Winnicott terms this *ego relatedness* and says that it is a form of ecstasy: the ego's pleasure at being with a mother who knows how to live with the

---

[1] In MP, pp. 29–36.

infant. In his essay 'The theory of the parent–infant relationship'(1960)[2], he addresses how the true self can come into being only through the mother's capacity to facilitate the infant's continuity of being: a relatively unbroken continuousness that enables idiom to unfold.

[2] In MP, pp. 37–55.

8

The Uses of Illusion

A dream is reality for a child, a reality in which parents are not ready
at hand. A small child dreaming of being in a school bus that goes
off road into a lake believes he is drowning. He calls for his mother,
and yet no one appears.

Most children know that a dream is not necessarily a safe or com-
forting world. Fear of the dark derives from encounters with the
ghosts that populate dream life. When we go off to sleep, these are
free to wander in and out of our mental life. The dark that frightens
the child is not simply the lights turned out for bedtime, it is also
the elimination of light that comes with closing our eyes and losing
consciousness.

In anticipation of this transition from the relative safety of the
mother's and father's domain to the world of sleep, where anything
can happen, the child may develop an intense love of an object
which must be present with him in these crucial minutes before the
journey into dreams.

This is a transitional time.

The transitional object represents an emerging ability to know
that the dream is illusion. The child cannot control it, and when
he wakes from it he cannot immediately distinguish dream from
reality. The blanket or teddy bear is a comrade, a compatriot in
the making of illusion during the day. Then, as he goes off into the
world of dreams, his companion goes with him. Few children go off
to sleep entirely alone.

Because the transitional object reflects the capacity for illusion-
making, it must be preserved as something very special. A friend
who enters the dream space with the child, a signifier of survival

Essential Aloneness. Christopher Bollas, Oxford University Press. © Christopher Bollas 2024.
DOI: 10.1093/oso/9780197683880.003.0008

and of pleasure, it bridges the chasm between the hallucinatory realm of dream and the imaginative life of the awakened mind. It must not be changed or laundered by the parent, because it is not entirely of this world. To alter it would mean altering the imaginary, whether in play or in dreams.

If we look at it this way, we may say that the transitional object represents the infant's experience of the function of illusion. The life knowledge of make-believe as intermediary between hallucination and objectivity helps the child go off to sleep. He brings with him the experience of the in-between, as he enters a world where he knows that this distinction of an in-between can be eradicated.

It may be that children who seem unusually invested in keeping the transitional object with them during the day are experiencing some anxiety about the safety of illusion. If there is an uncertainty about the place of the imaginative use of the object, its actual presence may supersede its representation of an experience. As the object in itself becomes highly invested with significance, the capacity it was meant to signify becomes less important.

Winnicott says the transitional object could be the thumb, it could be the mother, it could be the father, it could be hair, it could be music, it could be a sound. It could be anything. What he does not say, however, is that a child can be making use of transitional space and transitional phenomena without any object being present. We do not need the object to authorize the use of transitional space, but it becomes vital when the capacity for transitional experience is under some kind of threat.

In considering the function of illusion in his 1951 essay on transitional objects, Winnicott makes the important point that illusion originates for the infant by virtue of the mother's near 100% adaptation to his needs. The example he gives is that she creates the illusion that the breast is part of the infant's body. So if we return to the child going off to sleep with the transitional object, we could say that this object inherits the first illusion of the breast's presence. When the infant wakes from a frightening dream, this ever-present illusory breast comforts him when the mother is not there as a physical presence.

Winnicott writes that a good enough mother creates an illusion that the good breast is always there—even in the midst of the frightful dream—and by feeding is soothed. The infant when going back to sleep finds peace of mind has returned. Thus the capacity for use of the illusion emerges from the infant's experience of the mother's adaptation to his needs.

The original companion, therefore, is the breast. When the infant wakes from a nightmare, the awakening could be seen as a rejection or splitting-off of the persecutory inner objects. He says, 'No, this is not me. It is not my world', and sure enough along comes the breast to assure him that all is well. It delivers the infant from distress and transforms distress into gratification. It helps him move from a nightmare into a benign dream state.

Although an infant will have some mental representation of the good breast as an inner object, the value of the illusion of the seemingly ever-present breast rests not in its thing-corporeality, but in the process it provides. In the moments of distress and danger, we are saved by the miraculous intervention of the soothing object. The illusion becomes a sense of inner strength.

Illusion is the foundation of belief. In the course of childhood, through his use of the function of illusion—a stick becomes a rocket for exploring outer space—the child discovers the value of giving in to something that we might call faith. This involves making use of the maternal process. He knows that if he gives in to the belief that the rocket exists, he will not devolve into psychosis. We know that we can imagine safely because there will be a safe return from the imaginary. This remains an underlying principle of our existence.

You recall Winnicott's theory of the spatula and the period of hesitation. He noticed that if he put the spatula on the table between the baby and himself, the baby would look at it and then turn away. But then, apparently indifferent, he would return to look at the object again, start to drool and then try to get it into his mouth.

To some extent, when the patient sees the analyst he turns away. Lying on the couch with the analyst out of sight, he is free to create the analyst. So, built into the structure of psychoanalysis is the period of hesitation that Winnicott regards as fundamental to all infants in terms of object usage. In analysis the patient has the opportunity to create a subjective object, whereas in face-to-face psychotherapy, with the object always in sight, I think it is more difficult. In analysis, we get the feeling that the patient is creating us, inventing us, and generally enjoying the invention of this companion that is the analyst.

I recall the case of a little girl who was extremely inhibited. She drew a picture of her house in which there were many rooms, all neatly divided. In one room there was a television and in another there was a spider. She had some fears connected with watching television. It was frightening because there was some confusion between herself and the television programmes. The spider that she created was the only alive object in that house, and I think it represented her instinctual life. The spider was her way of expressing her instincts, and I thought that the therapist should celebrate this: 'Ah, a spider!' This would support the idea that instincts and the expression of instinctual life were important and valued in the evolution of her analysis.

Celebration of the analysand's communications is a form of interpretation.

9

Communicating/Not Communicating

'Original aloneness' is the being of the predependent infant. We have memories of it. One way to think about it is to imagine the internal space we carry with us to receive our feelings and thoughts. We know that much of our internal life is spent in subvocal conversations with ourself, but there are times when there are few if any conversations taking place in this theatre. It is then an empty chamber.

Original aloneness is a primary feeling that we carry with us throughout our life. As we approach death, our sense of it is informed by our history of original aloneness, which guides us back to pre-existence. Winnicott says that this inherent aloneness can be interfered with by anxiety and by psychopathological states, but it is generally a peaceful part of the personality.

Perhaps you can see why Winnicott values a particular kind of silence within the psychoanalytical session, one that is inhabited by essential aloneness. What an error it is to regard such silence as a resistance to speech when, in fact, it is the silent voice of being. The psychoanalytic setting and the experience of being alone in the presence of the analyst evoke inherent aloneness. It is unchanged and unchangeable, but it is now shared with the other. Both patient and analyst know primary aloneness, even if it will remain forever unthought.

What we are discussing has little to do with object-relating. In a certain kind of way, it comes close to Winnicott's concept of 'simple not-communicating.'[1] Here he is not implying something

---

[1] See 'Communicating and not communicating leading to a study of certain opposites' (1963) in MP, p. 183.

Essential Aloneness. Christopher Bollas, Oxford University Press. © Christopher Bollas 2024.
DOI: 10.1093/oso/9780197683880.003.0009

simple-minded, lacking depth. It is a living-out of something deep inside the core of the self, which through its form becomes a communicating, a transporting. As we shall see later on, this not-communicating has no intentionality; it is not part of an object relationship. It simply exists in its own space.

Freud's theory of endopsychic perception makes it possible to understand that we have some perception-memory of the evolution of our self, from unaliveness through primary aloneness into continuity of being. So do we have dreams or fantasies that recall this memory of psychic evolution, or that represent psychic structure itself?

There is a part of the unthought known that remains a secret even to ourselves, no matter how diligently we seek to know it. Winnicott addresses the organization of being prior to language, and he considers that elements of the true self can be elaborated through psychoanalysis, particularly through the lyrical formulations and specific idioms of free association and the dense, curious discourses in the transference and in the countertransference. However, each of us dies with only a small portion of our true self ever articulated.

Perhaps, in the end, the transitional object is the true self's only object. It reflects our idiom-in-being, and through the use of this object the character of the true self is given a metaphorical representation.

In his essay 'Communicating and not communicating leading to study of certain opposites', Winnicott examines the communication that takes place with our subjective objects. He says, 'in so far as the object is subjective, *so far is it unnecessary for communication with it to be explicit*' (MP182). He maintains that the non-communicating self reflects a personal core that is a true isolate.

It may be hard to ponder a communication with an isolated part of the self that is beyond knowing, but I think we know it from our own inner life. We are always in some relation to the part of ourself beyond consciousness, and there is a form of non-explicit communicating between our consciousness and our unconscious.

It is not intentional, it has no aim, and it will always be beyond analytical endeavour.

In my paper 'Ordinary regression to dependence'[2], I write about
mental processes that derive from the core of the self, and perhaps
there is some relation between these processes and Winnicott's idea
of the isolate self. In his essay Winnicott distinguishes between two
types of mother, the 'environment mother' and the 'object mother.'
The 'environment mother is human', says Winnicott and 'the object mother is more a thing'(MP182–3). There is intercommunica-
tion between infant and environment mother which is, as he says,
'subtle to a degree'(MP183). In a sense, it is not meaningful to talk
about a distinction between the 'environment mother' and the infant, but we could say that the intercommunicating between them
elaborates that communicating between the conscious part of ourself and primary aloneness.

Winnicott makes a distinction between simple not
communicating and a 'not-communicating that is active or
reactive'(MP183). He says that the first of these 'is like resting. It is
a state in its own right, and it passes over into communicating, and
reappears as naturally' (MP183). In other words, there is an oscil-
lation in our life between 'simple not communicating' and the wish
or the urge or the need to communicate.

He proceeds to make what is for me a very important connection
when he says 'one should be able to make a positive statement of
the healthy use of non-communication in the establishment of the
feeling of real'(MP184). This is one of the priorities in Winnicott's
approach to analysis: to provide conditions that enable the person
to experience his or her own inner sense of personal reality. To feel
real. Perhaps the most significant relating and communicating is
silent.

If we believe that non-communicating is a positive element, then
in an analysis it is important that this be allowed in order for the

---

[2] See *The Shadow of the Object*. London, Routledge, 2018. pp. 173–185.

patient to feel personally real and truly present within his analysis. Except when we are with somebody with whom we are deeply close, it is probably true for most of us that we are only completely relaxed when we are alone. The presence of the other invites work. In his clinical work, I think Winnicott tried to make it possible for the patient to achieve that state of total relaxation which can exist for the individual who is either alone, or alone in the presence of someone. And we know, patients who do not speak for a long time may feel apologetic. This is an indication of the strain they are under, and with some it can take a long time before they can feel at ease with not communicating. Winnicott writes:

> I would add that there is a direct development, in health, from this silent communicating to the concept of inner experiences that Melanie Klein described so clearly. (MP185)

He adds:

> I suggest that in health there is a core to the personality that corresponds to the true self of the split personality; I suggest that this core never communicates with the world of perceived objects, and that the individual person knows that it must never be communicated with or be influenced by external reality. (MP187)

This is a radical statement for a psychoanalyst to make. I know of nobody else in the history of psychoanalysis who has ever made this comment, and it may take us a very long time before we truly understand what he means.

10

Being and Potential Space

To begin our discussions for this week I shall review something of what we have studied thus far.

Winnicott believes that insofar as the child's continuity of being is concerned, there is nothing in his experiencing that is lost. In some form we remember everything, even though, as is certainly the case, most of what we know is unconscious.

Let me emphasize the significance of this point, the idea of remembering all of our experiencing. Some time before birth, the foetus has lived through an extraordinary transition from nonexistence into existence. At the point of such existing, Winnicott says that there is a primary aloneness which is the first basis of our life. We carry this with us always, and there is an area inside the self to which we can re-turn in order to experience it.

This essential aloneness may be viewed as the beginning of the continuity of our being, which is different from our sense of our aliveness. Being, in a sense, occurs within us but it seems not to be of our own possession, of our own making. It is more a quality, a universal.

The differentiation between 'being' and 'aliveness' may remind us of some important continental philosophy. This distinction exists in Heidegger and certainly in Sartre, who distinguishes between 'being in itself' and 'being for itself'. 'Being in itself' relates to Winnicott's concept of being, and therefore to primary aloneness. 'Being for itself' is an act: a development, a movement of the subject, and close to Winnicott's concept of aliveness. For both Sartre and Winnicott, being in itself is not historical, whereas being for

Essential Aloneness. Christopher Bollas, Oxford University Press. © Christopher Bollas 2024.
DOI: 10.1093/oso/9780197683880.003.0010

itself, and aliveness, are historical in that the subject creates his history.

Perhaps there are individuals, such as those who are profoundly autistic, who foreclose all features of human existing except for the sense of essential aloneness. It is a form of privacy, and when this is challenged by the other, the subject may withdraw his object cathexes in order to collect all of his personality into a kind of shelter for the total protection of his aloneness.

This suggests that we might reconsider the tendency of the autistic child to create such a protection as being a positive accomplishment. When we are with him, it is his radical solitude that is so striking. It can be so effective that we appear to have no bearing upon his presence at all.

Can Winnicott's idea of aloneness be extended to the subject's encounter with the speechless logic of the universal order that authorizes and governs the existence of organic life and inorganic movement? Perhaps our sense of affinity with the natural world is, in part, an endopsychic perception, through which we have a sense of affinity with the structure of life itself.

When aliveness first begins to emerge out of primary aloneness, this a purely somatic process that carries with it its own senses and memories. Winnicott describes 'the great changeover' from foetal life to existence in the outside world. This is something we assume.

At this point, I shall digress for a moment. We are in a particular moment in the history of psychoanalysis, in which a new liberation of sorts must take place. Amongst many other achievements, Freud liberated the sexuality of the child and of the hysterical woman. He enabled the psychoanalytical profession to understand the meaning of infantile sexuality and hysterical symptomatology. Klein liberated psychosis from the chains of prejudice. She made it possible for us to believe in the psychoanalysis of the psychotic person.

Because Freud liberated the child, he made it possible for all of us to contact the infant/child parts of ourselves. Similarly, Klein gave us access to our psychotic parts. It seems to me that what Winnicott is trying to do through metaphor and imagination is to liberate our self as foetus and infant. He encourages us to give thought to the psychic states of the foetus and to keep in mind that we have within us memories and structures of our being before our birth.

In *The Interpretation of Dreams*, Freud noted that when we sleep at night we assume a foetal position. Sleep occupies much of our life, and when we consider sleeping, and its relation to the dream, we are in a sense discussing foetal-self phenomena. There seems to be a resistance to the idea of the significance of a foetal life, but to help us overcome this we have not only Winnicott but also Bion.

In his extraordinary book *The Dawn of Oblivion*, Bion tries to create an imaginative space for foetal existence. In his emphasis on the elements of mental life rather than on personalities, he makes it possible to trace certain elements back to this pre-birth state. Maybe primary maternal preoccupation is based, to some extent, on the mother's unconscious memories of her own changeover from foetal to post-foetal life.

We have previously considered the next stage, in which the mother provides for the new baby the illusion that the world appears according to the infant's need. Eventually, through ordinary good enough mothering, she will gradually help him discover the limits of illusion, as she progressively declines to support his expectation of omnipotence. When the baby learns to crawl, and can move around independently in his environment, he discovers that the things he encounters don't move out of his way. He meets the inevitable resistance of ordinary objects.

It is significant that Winnicott never speaks of the mother's creating for the baby a *sense* of omnipotence. He says that she creates the *experience* of omnipotence. These are two very different states. To create experiences of omnipotence at the early stage is one function of the good enough mother. If a sense of omnipotence is the outcome, there has been a failure in good enough mothering.

Through continuous provision of illusion the mother creates a new space for the infant. This is a potential space, a place for experiencing, a 'third area'. The other two areas are the purely internal world and the purely external world. Naturally, one of the first tasks of a child's infancy is to learn to distinguish between inner and outer reality. In the course of this gradual differentiation, the mother introduces objects (such as her breast) at the moment of infant need, and this provision of illusion is the precursor to the capacity to use potential space.

Potential space becomes a transitional area when the infant feels at ease in possessing his first 'not-me' object, and there is a pleasure in the object's thingness that allows him to invent his meaning for it. Remember, it is his possession. He designates it as such, and his ownership of it allows him to give it his own meaning. It is this that enables him to act out his use of it as an object.

Winnicott refers to this space as 'the area of experiencing'. 'Experiencing' is a special word for Winnicott. It is not purely internal, like phantasy; it is composed of the subject's imaginative encounter with the actual world. This applies also in a dream, when the actual is represented in disguised form.

Winnicott talks about 'dependence', and in doing so he is emphasizing the signified, not the signifier. He maintains that it is of value to note how and why the infant is *actually* dependent. Babies and toddlers cannot manage on their own, and adults need to keep in mind what we no doubt need to lose: that we actually have been completely dependent beings.

This was Winnicott's continual critique of Klein. He believed that she simply did not adequately appreciate the infant's dependence, not on an internal object but on an actual mother who was needed to preserve his existence. Because of this, the baby is affected by the nature of his environment, which can give him a sense of confidence or precariousness. This is determined by the cumulation of experiences which add up into memories—as patterns derived from lived experience—so that by the end of the first year of life, we may speak of babies who are confident and babies who feel vulnerable.

For the psychoanalyst, the simplicity of this fact can be somewhat annoying. It comes as a disappointment to the complex parts of ourselves that are Freudian, Kleinian, and Lacanian, because it denies us the opportunity to exercise our minds or show off our talents. I think this is partly why Winnicott's work can be an object of contempt amongst certain analysts, particularly those who reject the idea of the external environment having fundamental significance.

But especially during the first year of life, it is crucial. A six-year-old boy might be living in a poverty-stricken family, but if he had a good first year, then he will have a sense of himself and he will be able to defend himself against considerable environmental disappointment. In his state of absolute dependence, the infant inevitably develops a feel of the predictable as mother establishes a pattern of care.

Winnicott's emphasis on the idea of the building of a self differs from Klein's view. For her, psychic health is a matter of good internal objects predominating over persecutory ones, based on the success of splitting, idealization, and eventual reparation. She believes that the internal world derives fundamentally from the balance in the infant between the life and death instincts. Although she does acknowledge a function for the mother in this situation, her focus is on the internal psychic work of the infant. For Klein, and also for Freud, the object is fundamentally created out of the infant's instinctual urges. Winnicott, on the other hand, emphasizes the value of lived experience within the infant/mother couple. Although the object has instinctual status, it is part of the relation to the mother.

Winnicott refers to 'object presenting'; there is no comparable idea in Freudian or Kleinian psychoanalysis. For Winnicott it is relevant to the infant's inner life to note how and when the mother presents him with objects (first the breast, cot, or spoon; later it might be crayons, books, or toys). Her function as the presenter of objects is part of her task of sustaining the value of transitional experiences for the child and of facilitating the eventual use of cultural objects.

In fact, child psychologists have always paid attention to this issue, albeit from a rather different perspective. Much of academic child psychology is based upon the evolution of the child's cognitive development, and this includes the use of objects. Winnicott, who during his career observed some 30,000 mother/child couples, regarded the way in which the mother presented objects to a child as very important. Some mothers would present objects in such a way as to cultivate the child's true self, but there were others who were uninterested or who demanded that the child accept her choice of object.

Naturally, this view suggests something about psychoanalytical technique, not in black and white terms but as a matter of emphasis. Winnicott maintains that the success of an analytical session depends very much on the analyst's skill in preserving the potential space: presenting interpretations as objects to the patient, at the right time and in the correct manner.

In Winnicott's writings, we find rather few references to the patient's destructive envy or to negative transference that disables the analyst. Indeed, given his extraordinarily creative way of considering and reconsidering a patient, it would be quite hard to imagine his mind being disabled by anyone. He certainly leaves us with the feeling that if some patients seem to be beyond us, this is because we have failed to reach them.

A baby's requirements in the dependent state are very simple. There are physiological needs: he might need to be moved in order to be warmer or cooler, to have softer clothing, to be carried about if he is in distress. At a more subtle level, the baby may need to feel the mother's breathing cadence or hear her mother's heartbeat. He is therefore dependent on the mother's capacity to notice his needs, to have developed inside her a wealth of maternal knowledge, built up out of her own infancy and her life experiences thereafter. The infant needs her to be in the right mood, or frame of mind, to adapt herself to him, to have a good enough way of touching him.

Many years ago I tried to imagine what this experience of dependence would be like for the infant. It is a curious situation because, as we know, the infant is quite cognitively gifted but is nonetheless helpless. I proposed that we term the mother the 'transformational object' because she transforms the infant's state of being, both psychically and somatically. Each of us has been the recipient of thousands of primary transformations during the state of absolute dependence, and I think we have a memory of this that is reflected in our search for such an object in adult life. The mother as transformational object exists in external reality, but she is known at first by the infant not as an object but as a process of alteration in his being. So in other words, an external object is experienced as an internal process. I think this emphasis follows Winnicott's tradition of thinking of mental, psychic, and self evolution as a process that in some respects involves two people.

I believe that the term 'intersubjectivity' is not quite right here. In the world of the infant and the mother, we should perhaps make more use of Bion's language, in terms of the elements of mental life being communicated back and forth. At this point we cannot meaningfully talk about personalities or whole objects. The mother's ability to meet the infant's needs during dependence are crucial. We might assume this to be a rather ordinary accomplishment, but Winnicott reminds us that when a mother fails, the infant experiences certain profound anxieties.

He lists four of these anxieties:

1) Going to pieces.
2) Falling forever.
3) Having no relationship to the body.
4) Having no orientation.

(MP58)

With good enough mothering these momentary traumas can be changed into positive experiences. Going to pieces can be transformed into relaxation and restfulness. Falling forever can be transformed into the thrills of being carried and the adventures of being moved. The sense of dying, dying, and dying can be transformed into a blissful delight of being alive. Losing all hope of refinding contact can be transformed into a sense of assurance that, even when he is alone, the baby has someone who cares.

It is important to understand that these are an infant's experience of the object. Much of what he feels and thinks about himself will metaphorize the mother's handling of him. If he is left to disintegrate, he may experience this as his due. He is meant to fall apart. Winnicott's perspective suggests that an adult patient's sense of disintegration may be a memory of the repeated experience of falling to pieces as an infant.

The Kleinian view of this situation considers only the internal phenomenon: the infant attacks the breast due to an increase in the quantity of hate; the object is split; it achieves a malevolent status and it attacks the infant from within. Winnicott would not disagree with this. A mother who fails her infant during his absolute dependence on her would sponsor this sort of internal destructive work, but such disintegration can, in his view, never be divorced from the mother's handling of the situation. A good enough mother will recover the fractured infant. Winnicott's repeated emphasis on the role of the mother in the infant's experience has its correlate in his view of analytic technique. The analyst aims to involve the patient in the analysis with the right doses of holding, object presenting, and playing.

I have suggested previously that the child inherits the mother's technique of nurturance, which becomes his own way of managing himself internally, as an object. In other words, in varying degrees the infant structuralizes the maternal process into an ego procedure. Such internalizations involve the subject in some kind of relation to himself as an object. This need not be a consciously objectifying act—the adult may not be speaking to himself. The internalization of the good enough mother can manifest itself in the unconscious assumptions of being and relating that constitute this person's idiom in life or in living. And what about the father? Is an infant not also the father's object? Does he not also affect the baby? Of course, he certainly does. The extent to which the father's processing of the infant is also internalized to achieve eventual structuralization as an ego procedure will depend on how much time he devotes to infant care.

In the beginning, in the life of the neonate and young infant, the true self develops gradually from simple 'being' into a representational inner world supported by the maternal process. This early period in the history of the subject occurs predominantly prior to that internal dynamic world in which instincts, needs, and wishes sponsor or assume primary authorship of the child's inner life.

The ego evolves out of its internalization of the mother's processes. The one inherits the other. Where mother was, there shall ego be.

To this schema we must add another system of demand, the demand that the object world makes upon the mind for work. Parenthetically, to me this is the most important aspect of Winnicott's revision of Kleinian object relations theory. For Klein, the demands made upon the mind for work come only from within the infant. Nowhere in her writings will you find references to any demand upon the mind for work created by the other. When she discusses a mother who may not be good enough, she does so only from the point of a resulting increase in the forces of hate inside the infant. She does not mention the character, the personality, the idiom of the other as it makes a demand upon the child to think what is taking place.

Yet the actions and the characters of the mother and father demand mental work from the infant. When the mother withdraws the breast in the middle of a feed in order to go and turn off the stove, this act becomes a demand upon the infant's mind. He must work to process this.

Thus, the psyche is an intermediate area between the mute demands of the soma and the complex actions of others. The internal object world is a field of relations between two different systems of demand, one biological, the other social. Somewhere in between, however, is the true self, an idiom of potential, that exists from before birth and that influences and partially determines psychic organization.

11

Object Relating

Yesterday I considered the fact of dependence. This does not insult the infant but serves him, initially, in his unquestioning belief in the mother's magic. In fact, paradoxically, it is not that the infant believes in the mother; he believes in the results of his own absolute need. The first outcome of this is the mother's breast. The infant, at this stage, does not know that the breast arrives out of the sensitive timing of the mother.

This need is not a thoughtful expression but an instinctual demand. It brings the object (breast) which is then destroyed (emptied). When need and demand from inside the body bring the object to the baby's mouth for destruction, the infant transforms an external object into an internal one.

There are several transformations involved here:

1) An internal demand is transformed into a body movement or a cry. (This is the Freudian theory of psychical representation.)
2) The infant's psychic representation is transformed into the object's corporeality.
3) The corporeality of the object (the breast) is transformed back to an inner state.

So an inner, somatic demand (instinctual urge) drives the baby to represent the demand, which seemingly creates a corporeal object, the breast, which goes into the body as both a substance and a feeling. This inner object is not simply mental; it has a somatic base. This substantiality is one way of describing the process of

Essential Aloneness. Christopher Bollas, Oxford University Press. © Christopher Bollas 2024.
DOI: 10.1093/oso/9780197683880.003.0011

incorporation and a means of differentiating it from introjection. The new inner state is a mix of the object's substance (the milk), and the state it brings (gratification).

Having gained meaning via these transformations, the object now has a psychic potential. Through incorporation the subject feels the trace of a substantial relation to the other, through the breast-object. Incorporation involves the senses, far more so than introjection. Let's relate this idea to the clinical situation. When the patient is internalizing the sound of the analyst's voice, the smell of the analyst, and the visual elements of the room, when he feels the physical sensation of touching the couch and being held by it, this is an incorporative mode of internalization. It is based on sensation.

All patients form incorporative internalizations of the psychoanalyst. Incorporation may be more primitive than introjection, but it is not true to say that it functions in adults only at a psychotic level. The sensational elements of incorporation are present in all our lives. For example, when we look at paintings, when we listen to music, this has an incorporative element because it involves a sensational relation to the object.

However, when the psychoanalyst makes an interpretation that sponsors the patient's conscious thinking about the content, this is a matter of introjection. The patient is taking in elements of mental life that do not have a primarily sensational connection, such as the perception of personality. It can be important to know the difference between these two modes of internalization.

In clinical work, we encounter patients who may be incorporating us but are not introjecting us.

Substantiality is a feature of incorporation. But even at a very early stage of development, the baby begins to sense the mother as a gratifying presence. Winnicott writes:

> We see the interesting process of the absorption into the individual child of the child-care elements, those which could be

called supporting ego elements. The relationship between this absorption of the environment and the introjective processes with which we are already familiar provides great interest. (MP126–7)[1]

This is important because Winnicott is suggesting that the baby takes in the mother's technique of care. This is an act of introjection. An infant who does not progress beyond the incorporative mode of internalization will not be able to introject the maternal care system, and this can lead to a serious deficiency in ego capability.

But what does the infant absorb? It is not, of course, simply the milk or the experience of the breast and the relation to the nipple; it is also the maternal idiom. Experiences such as the mother's sense of timing, her sense of embodiment (softness or hardness), her sense of gratification (whether she hurries to finish a feed or lingers with the infant), and her sense of aggression, are internalized by the infant.

How do we understand the meeting of two true selves: infant and mother? As the mother adapts to the infant's true self, facilitating the articulation of his idiom, she also enables him to exist within hers. I believe that this absorption of the maternal processes of care matriculates into an internal care system that becomes part of the infant's ego.

I wonder whether we need to alter somewhat our psychoanalytical concept of object relating. When psychoanalysts discuss object relations theory, they are usually talking about the subject's internalization of its objects. In other words, they are considering the experience of one person. When we want to focus on the dialectic between mother and infant, perhaps we need to use the term *subject relations theory*[2] in order to highlight the interplay between two subjectivities.

---

[1] See "Classification: Is there a psycho-analytic contribution to psychiatric classification?" in MP, pp. 124–139.
[2] An idea I proposed in *Forces of Destiny*.

I have called this mutual effect 'informative object relating'[3]. The object will become a part of the subject according to the subject's willingness to be informed by it. The word 'inform' generally means to communicate an idea to another, but if you break the word down it implies the act of forming within the other. You in-form: you create the form within. So, with this phrase 'informative object relating', I am playing with the idea that communicating involves the object's in-forming of the subject.

If we think about the respective approaches of Fairbairn and Klein, we see an important difference of view. Klein argues that the infant endeavours to take in the good breast in order to preserve the good. Fairbairn argues the opposite: that the baby introjects the bad breast in order to control its persecutory elements. Neither theoretician suggests that the issue of whether the baby coheres around the good or the bad breast may have a good deal to do with the quality of the object presented to him.

If the breast is good, this reflects the mother's mothering, so we can say that the baby takes in the good enough mother. There will then exist in this person a primary good object. If a baby has not had good enough mothering, he may be left with a primary bad internal object that he will need to try to control.

In fact, of course, things cannot be divided in this simple way. There are good enough mothers, not good enough mothers, and many versions of a mix between the two. Infants are informed by complex objects. An informing object does not displace the true self. It is more like an internal environment in which the infant will generally experience a mixture of reception and refusal. I am sure infants deal differently with each in-forming object, and it would be too simplistic to say that a mother who provides the infant with an unfavourable environment will inevitably produce a disturbed child.

---

[3] In 2016 this will be defined as 'interformality'. See Christopher Bollas, *The Christopher Bollas Reader*, ed. Arne Jemstedt, London, Routledge, 2011.

What about the baby's in-forming of the mother? For various possible reasons, some babies seem incapable of being soothed. It may be that a difficulty originated in the womb or in the transition from foetal life to birth. Then there is the inherited factor in the constitution of the baby's idiom. Winnicott calls this the 'inherited potential', and I think this is wise phrasing indeed. It may take a lifetime to assess how much of this true self has been allowed to come into human being, and how much is forestalled, causing the person to live from the false self.

Winnicott claims that his experience of working with mothers and their babies has enabled him to see patterns of relating to objects established in infancy. He finds that mothers nurture by intuition, and that it is an act of violence when frustrated nurses or carers shove a bottle into the baby's mouth which can stimulate a gag reflex. He argues that babies need time before they can begin to search around for objects. And when they find one they may want to linger with it, engaging it in a form of play.

As the analyst, it can be difficult to find a part of oneself that can observe what happens within the intermediate area of experiencing. Of course, this involves empathy: imagining both who we are for the patient, and the object that we are inside them. But it also involves observing the interplay between analyst and patient, taking notice of the ambiance, the environment created between the two.

One of the tasks of an analysis is to enable the move from purely internal object relations to object relating. Part of our difficult task is to find a place within ourself from which we can observe ourself with our patient at play. When we see two children playing we are observing object relating; we discover two people creating an area in which the two of them can be. They are creating their culture. And the same is true of a psychoanalysis. We can become so preoccupied with intense, ferocious thinking about internal objects that we have no room in ourselves for the observation of object relating.

I recently met with a former patient. We sat opposite one another. After twenty seconds or so she frowned and turned to 'serious issues' that she had come to talk to me about.

After about 45 minutes, having presented five or six serious issues, she lapsed into silence. I recognized it as the same silence that had been a feature of her analysis. I hadn't seen her for some years, and now I found myself wanting to try to figure out what it was that created this silence. It was something that I had known, but that I had not been able to think about with her until now.

I realized that we had created an atmosphere in the analysis in which the two of us were trying far too hard. She struggled to bring the material from the unconscious; I tried too hard to analyse her. The very seriousness of our effort destroyed the intermediate area where play and phantasy could have a life of its own. I said, 'I think I know what our problem is. You and I have been far too serious together.'

We can say that there were projective identifications on her part, and I'm sure that's true, but I felt it was important that I take responsibility for my part in this. It was a very important moment for both of us, and her face registered her feelings in a way that I had never seen during the analysis because she had been on the couch, out of my sight.

This experience comes to my mind because it illustrates the difference between the analysis of internal object relations, and of object relating. If a patient is capable of object relating, and the analyst fails at this level—as I had with this patient—then I believe an analysis cannot fully evolve.

Object relating is multifaceted. Sometimes mother and baby simply gaze at one another. The mother may rock the infant. The infant may smile at the mother. The mother may jostle the baby for the fun of it. The baby may express surprise and the mother may reassure the infant. All the elements of advanced human relating are here in some form. It is an in-formative relation in which the mother contributes substantially to her form within the baby. She does not create the infant, but she does process him, and he in turn takes this processing into himself.

Both Freud and Klein tend to assume a neutral external object. Klein gives us valuable ways to think about the possible formations of our interactions with internal objects, but in Winnicott's concept of object relations the specific nature of the other has a profound effect on the child. He stresses the interaction of two different personalities upon one another.

This cannot be simply dismissed by claiming that the object is merely a product of the infant's perception, and it therefore exists only intrapsychically. Of course, we see with our own eyes, no one else's. But if we are hit on the head by a falling apple, this fact has its own integrity, force, and validity, which cannot be extinguished by saying, 'This is how I perceived what happened.' What we make of our experience is naturally a vital feature of intrapsychic reality, but this internal meaning-making cannot exist without lived experience.

In fact we can call upon Klein's theory of projective identification to make this very point. The Kleinians have placed great emphasis on how the analysand projects valued or destructive parts of the self into the analyst. These projections can have a profound effect on the analyst, shaping him internally in such a way as to influence his internal life. Indeed, we know from this theory that a patient's projective identifications are often so powerful and effective that the analyst acts them out, often through interpretation.

This theory of projective identification is the most radical, some would say extreme, theory of the effect of one real person upon another. It does not restrict itself to endopsychic effects, the play of internal objects. It addresses how the actual speech, behaviour, and interpersonal actions of one person enter into the internal world of another, directly affecting the recipient's mental life.

The Kleinians, to my continuing surprise, apply this very radical theory only to the patient's effect on the analyst. They do talk of counter-projective identification—actions by the analyst based upon the force of the original projective identification from the patient—but they do not take into account that the analyst acts unconsciously on the patient via their own projective identification.

And they do not acknowledge the role and function of projective identification in the mother's relation to the baby. This is all the more surprising because there is probably no relation in which projective identification is more active than in the mother's administrations to her infant. As she cares for him, she puts many parts of herself into the baby. She projects and identifies in order to imagine the baby, to speak to him, to reply, to surprise, to soothe, to enjoy. To whom is she speaking? Is she not speaking to the infant part of herself, which is hopefully attuned with the infant's state of self?

In my view, we can say that one of the reasons a borderline patient feels so fractured and anguished is that he had to carry split off fragments of the mother's personality. We can think of depressive disorders as biased by the mother's projective identification of destructive parts of herself, attacking the baby as an object, causing a loss of self-esteem and precipitating a prolonged inner battle within the infant. Similarly, a schizoid element could prevail due to the mother's seductive over-invasiveness as she eroticized the baby, who defended himself from this erotics by decathecting the object world and going into hiding.

The true self is not formed by the mother, but she can forestall or facilitate it. I have sketched out some of the possible effects of the object to give us a way of thinking about the actions of the other upon the psyche. The psyche, the internal world, is an intermediate area between the somatic and the actual, between the biological and the sociological. It is here that these two separate yet dialectically linked processes come together. Freud taught us that the instinct creates its inner object in the psyche, but what we have seen is that the object is also informative in and of itself.

The child mediates, and in this mediation he creates his own inner life. This may involve a neurotic, borderline, schizoid, or psychotic solution to the inner balances and figurations of the meeting-up of the objects of soma and of the actual.

12

The Use of an Object

Perhaps none of Winnicott's concepts has aroused as much suspicion or fascinated alarm as his idea of the use of an object. However, this is an integral part of his theory of object relationships.

To begin to understand the extraordinary sophistication behind Winnicott's thinking of this idea, we need to start with his differentiation between two mothers. He writes in 1963[1]:

> [I]t seems possible to use these words 'object-mother' and 'environment-mother' in this context to describe the vast difference that there is for the infant between two aspects of infant-care, the mother . . . who wards off the unpredictable and who actively provides care in handling and in general management. (MP75)

These two mothers receive different infant attitudes. The environment mother 'receives all that can be called affection and sensuous co-existence' (MP75–6), while the object mother 'becomes the target for excited experience backed by crude instinct-tension' (MP76). It is one of the functions of the environment mother to hold the infant, particularly during his attacks on the object mother.

Unlike Klein, Winnicott does not assume that these two mothers are separate because the infant splits the object. At this early stage, Winnicott believes there is no clear distinction yet for the baby between what is intended and what actually takes place. The splitting associated with the good and the bad object comes later, and is a split of a different order. Winnicott does accept Klein's concept of

---

[1] See 'The development of the capacity for concern' in MP, pp. 73–82.

Essential Aloneness. Christopher Bollas, Oxford University Press. © Christopher Bollas 2024.
DOI: 10.1093/oso/9780197683880.003.0012

the need to keep the two separate, but for him, the environment mother and the object mother divide not according to good and bad, but according to two separate systems of needs: firstly, the need for quiet and holding; secondly, the need for an object of attack. The concept of the object mother is best illustrated, according to Winnicott, by the infant's attack on the breast during feeding. The feed is a cannibalistic attack—a form of ruthlessness—which the mother survives.

It is important to keep in mind that before the infant has any sense of the object's survival of his attacks, the object is surviving. This is crucial in understanding the complex evolution in the emotional progression of the individual that is based on the dialectic of inner experience and object relating. It is the many experiences of the ruthless attack on the breast, unchallenged by the mother, which gradually enables the infant to make an important discovery: the object survives!

The split between the environment mother and the object mother is not determined by the infant; it is a divide maintained by the mother herself. Indeed, it is her act of facilitation that allows the infant to use splitting successfully. This idea represents an emphasis that is different from Klein's. She maintains that a split is created by the infant to prevent the good and bad objects from coming together. The infant uses the force of love to create a good object, the good breast, which is idealized in order to protect him against persecutory attack by the bad breast. The eventual arrival of the depressive position is then a kind of necessary inner catastrophe: the ideal object must mingle with the bad in order to become internally real.

This is the Kleinian position. Winnicott would not entirely disagree with this conceptualization, but he adds that the mother sustains the split and, we can add, enjoys it.

His way of thinking places less emphasis on the libido, or psychic force, expended by the infant in creating the ideal. By actively sustaining this ideal state herself, the mother frees him to use his energy for other purposes. The good, sustaining mother is therefore not the creation of the infant, not a projective identification, but a mutual creation. It is an actual living experience, sustained for each by the other.

The environment mother also enjoys the infant's attack, and in this respect she takes pleasure in his aggression. This pleasure is part of what we have termed informative object relating. When the mother communicates to the infant her pleasure in his attacks, she implicitly supports his right to this form of expression. The French idea of *jouissance—the* universal right to ecstasy—comes out of this experience. Indeed, through Winnicott's theory we can see the context in which *jouissance* emerges. This inalienable right is supported by the environment mother who says 'this full breast is for both of us to enjoy'.

As the breast needs to be emptied, there is a biological necessity which underwrites the spirit of *jouissance*. The breast will be emptied by the infant's attack, and this gives pleasure both to the subject and to the other. This sequence (urge-attack-pleasure) is a complex joining up of biological need, ego requirements, and object usage.

There is no mother in Freud's theory of instinct fusion. Yet we cannot fully understand this theory unless we appreciate the function and the role of the mother, as it is she who facilitates the fusion of instincts. In Klein's thinking, there is a mother who does not like the infant's use of her body. It is rare in the Kleinian literature to find an analyst who interprets the patient's omnipotence or denigration as a form of pleasure. It is generally seen, instead, as something aimed at destroying the psychoanalyst's mind.

In this respect, Paula Heimann thought very differently about object relating. I shall never forget her words when she was supervising my work with a hysterical female patient. She said, 'I hope you let this woman destroy you. She needs to destroy you. And I hope you two find pleasure in her destruction of you.' *Jouissance* depends on the capacity of the mother to translate existential thrills into an appetite for pleasure and the valuing of objects.

We can see how this early aspect of the infant's experience develops into the capacity for adult intercourse, in which each understands and takes pleasure in the other's destruction of the object of excitement. This relates to the man's experience of the woman's pleasure as he penetrates her vagina, and to the woman's use of the man's penis, which she controls and then destroys through the man's orgasm. He arouses her into the impersonality of her own instincts. She loses herself, given over to the sensational logic of her soma as it directs her body. Erogenous zones demand touch and destruction, and all the while she is using the penis, which she holds in her vagina, applying and loosening her vaginal muscles, moving her pelvic position to use the penis differently. All of this is part of her use of an object which is hers in this moment to use and to destroy. Lovers take ecstatic pleasure in erotic destruction which ends in *la petite mort*.

Here is another example of the effect of the object upon the subject. In the Freudian model, instinct is endopsychic, emerging from within the body to create its own object. A man or woman, existing more or less alone, experiences genital urges as the instinctual drive is met with images of a desired sexual object. At some point the person goes searching for the object of desire.

However, we know that this is not the only way in which instinctual representations happen. A person might be sitting quietly, reading a book, with no instincts active within the self, when an attractive person unexpectedly walks into the room and an instinctual urge is summoned by their sudden appearance. In other words, just as the id creates a demand upon the mind for work, so too does the other.

Of course, in a sense this is why instinct is felt to be destructive: it is no longer possible to read the book. Instincts shake the body into arousal, whether we like it or not. There is ruthlessness in the impersonality of instincts when they are evoked by the other. If we are alone and an instinctual urge emerges, we may be able to banish it for a while in order to fulfil the need to carry on working. We can generally delay gratification. However, if the object is sitting in a chair across the room, winking at you, it may not be possible to ignore it and restore solitude.

If the environment mother does not support the infant's *jouissance*, if she refuses his attack, then the infant will be unable to destroy the object. He then loses the opportunity to communicate to her his inner need and his state of aliveness. Interrelating with a real external person may then be replaced by internal object relating, as the refusing mother sponsors the infant's creation of persecutory representations of herself. If the infant imagines being torn to pieces by the internal mother, a malicious circle is sustained by his inability to express and detoxify hate through actual object usage. Hate is now enacted within the psyche and immediately creates its counterpart in the object, which hates with equivalent force.

What is missing here? It is the function of the environment mother to mediate conflict. When this does not happen, a destructive split occurs for the infant between the environment mother and the object mother. Indeed, she may dissociate an element of herself, splitting off a feature of the container to put it out of the infant's reach. He can find these objects only within his mind, and they are of little use. Indeed, the intensity of internal objects in this situation testifies to the breakdown of object relating.

Klein says that infants recover from the paranoid schizoid position through the increasing internalization of a good object. This is seen as a triumph of the life instincts, and I'm sure this is correct in terms of the inevitable momentary breakdowns in the infant/mother relationship. When the mother fails the infant, the environment mother disappears and the infant experiences the paranoid schizoid position, but he will generally recover from this through the return of the good enough mother.

All infants at times suffer temporary breakdown into the paranoid schizoid position, as do all adults. When a breakdown occurs in object relating, each of us experiences minor madness and the work of recovery from the persecutory moment. This is not serious as long as we understand that such breakdown is ordinary.

Klein emphasizes the recognition of the fact that the loved object and the hated object are one and the same, and that this leads the infant to want to make reparation for the damage. This theory puts guilt as a primary force in the life of the one-year-old infant. To me, however, what motivates bringing together the two objects of love and hate is not guilt. The driving force in the integration of the object is pleasure. It is pleasurable to hate the object. It does not sponsor persecutory guilt unless the mother refuses the pleasure of the baby. If we look at an infant of twelve, fifteen, or twenty-four months, the driving factor of pleasure in the relation is something that we can see very clearly.

13

The Vitality of Aggression

Yesterday I discussed the priority Winnicott places on external object relating as formative of internal object relations. Of course, it is not a one-way process. Internal object relations also inform external object relating, but in infancy the nature of relations with external objects is more crucial to the internal world than it will be later. From the oedipal period onwards, the intrapsychic achieves a kind of parity of force with the intersubjective, and the other becomes less influential, less intensely informative.

In my view, psychoanalysis has been mistaken in separating aggression from pleasure. According to Winnicott we can trace aggression back to the beginnings of foetal movement, because the beginnings of motility are forms of aggression. Indeed, aggression is 'muscle erotism' (MP74)—establishing a template that links the pleasure of movement with aggression.

He believes that there is a hereditary factor, but also that babies are affected by the way in which they come into birth. He maintains that if one infant is aggressive and another appears not to be, in fact 'each has the same problem.' It is simply that the two children are dealing with their fear of aggressive impulses in different ways. He writes:

> If we look and try to see the start of aggression in an individual what we meet is the fact of infantile movement. This even starts before birth, not only in the twistings of the unborn baby, but also in the more sudden movements of limbs that make the mother say she feels a quickening. A part of the infant moves and by moving meets something. (DD93)

Essential Aloneness. Christopher Bollas, Oxford University Press. © Christopher Bollas 2024.
DOI: 10.1093/oso/9780197683880.003.0013

It is through movement that self meets object. The foetus comes up against something and discovers a resistance to it, a necessary and inevitable factor in object relating. Aggression that is not resisted is no longer pleasurable, because there is no meeting. The infant needs the resistance of the mother, who converts motility into pleasurable mutuality.

I make a distinction between celebration of the analysand and the idea of resistance, although I think there is a compatibility between the two ideas. It is possible to celebrate the patient's articulation of aggression and at the same time to resist the implications of the particular internal object formation. In other words, if the patient's internal representation of the analyst is, let us say, that he is impotent or an idiot, the analyst does not have to celebrate this by agreeing with it—'Oh, yes of course you are right, I'm an idiot.' Instead, the analyst might say, with a certain affectivity, 'Oh, so you think I'm an idiot! So maybe you'd like to tell me off!' This comment expresses a resistance on the analyst's part but at the same time it is a celebration of the patient's right to aggression.

We should remind ourselves of the mother's psychic experience of foetal movement, and the variety of possible responses to the question of infant motility. Does she enjoy it when the foetus kicks? Does she feel proud and pleased, even though it may hurt? Does it bring a smile to the father's face when he feels this movement that is a sign of life? Or does the mother cry out in pain or swear at the foetus and complain to the father, who must then see the baby as attacking the mother and damaging her? Does he feel he must protect and console his wife?

Note how different these two reactions are. In the first situation, the parents celebrate the infant's right of movement, her separateness, so later there will be a freedom in the child's use of objects rather than a fear that her energetic impulses are harmful to the other. In the second case, they see her primarily as an aggressive object inside the mother, harming her body and her peace of mind. In this case, aggression is interpreted as destructiveness and the object withdraws, compelling the infant to alter the nature of her object cathexes. This object is then internalized, and this can be the basis for a paranoid schizoid position.

Winnicott writes: 'We can see that these early infantile hittings lead to a discovery of the world that is not the infant's self, and to the beginnings of a relationship to external objects' (DD94). In other words, the child discovers the object through movement, and this leads to 'the beginnings of exploration' and is part of the 'clear distinction between what is the self and what is not the self' (DD94).

I wish to stress here that the child is discovering the object through action, not through the articulation of unconscious phantasy. There is a difference between experience gained through direct relation to the actual object world and experience that is fundamentally intrapsychic and internal. It is Winnicott's view that aggression lived through object relating is valuable. He says that the infant both creates and magically destroys the object as he moves from creation of the subjective object to discovery of the objective object.

It can be traumatic for the infant to be faced too prematurely with the limits of her magical thinking. This is where maternal care is so important, as the mother helps the infant come to terms with the shock of the world beyond the infant's omnipotent control. Winnicott writes:

> If time is allowed for maturational processes, then the infant becomes able to be destructive and becomes able to hate and to kick and to scream instead of magically annihilating that world. In this way, *actual aggression is seen to be an achievement.* (DD98)

So, to translate this to the clinical situation: if we interpret aggression in the transference as an attack on the projection of a part of the mother, or father, or self into the analyst, then we are attacking the positive value of aggression itself. Furthermore, it compels the patient back into a paranoid schizoid position. It is important to bear in mind that in this situation it is the analyst who is promoting this split. It is crucial in clinical work to be able to differentiate primary aggression from true destructiveness. For Winnicott, aggression against the object in the transference is an achievement.

By allowing herself to be the object of the child's aggression when he is still under the sway of magical convictions, the mother enables the child to work through aggressive impulses in an expressive manner. They are represented as they are; the child does not have the conviction that his aggression is wrong or bad. This is an important transition facilitated by the mother as she helps the infant move into object use.

Here we see the positive function of externalization. For too long we have had a negative idea of the process of externalization because we have focused so much on projection and projective identification. In Winnicott we see the value of this process of moving inner states into object relating. We must accept the projections of a patient in order to facilitate the movement of their internal world into the analytical experience. If we interpret projections in the transference every time they occur, we defeat the patient's efforts to move from a schizoid world into object relating, and we risk conveying that the only way out of this position is through guilt and continuous reparation to the object that is damaged by his projections.

Now this is strange. Think of the mother and the baby, or the mother and the young child. How do infants become children, and children become adolescents? This is possible because the mother implicitly accepts the child's projections without interpretation. We could say healthy infancy and childhood is a continuous acting out, a continuous externalization that is essential to the free articulation of the true self. Winnicott writes (1939 in 'Aggression'):

As compared with magical destruction, aggressive ideas and behaviour take on a positive value, and hate becomes a sign of civilization, when we keep in mind the whole process of the emotional development of the individual, and especially the earliest stages. (DD98–9)

This is an extraordinary statement. It is the first time to my knowledge that an analyst says that hate is a sign of civilization. How radically different this is from both Freud and Klein.

Winnicott maintains that the capacity to hate signifies trust in the mother, the father, and society; trust in the wisdom of the parents who know that for the child to mature favourably, he needs to destroy objects in order to create them. 'Aggression is part of the primitive expression of love', he writes in the 1950s, and he refers to aggression as 'the first love impulse.' (TP205).To begin, before the infant develops a capacity for concern, he is in a stage of ruthlessness or 'pre-ruth' (TP211). In this pre-ruth stage he does not aim to harm the object. It is simply that 'his excited love includes an imaginative attack on the mother's body' (TP206), and this is part of the expression of love. I think the mother mirrors this when she says to the child, 'I love you so much I could eat you all up.'

Winnicott distinguishes three patterns of aggression:

1) A healthy pattern in which 'the environment is constantly discovered and rediscovered because of motility'[1] (TP211). This affirms for the individual that he is emerging from the centre or the core of the self.

2) A reactive pattern in which the individual is impinged upon by the environment. This sets up a series of responses to impingements which means that he must withdraw in order to rest: 'Motility is then only experienced as a reaction to impingement' (TP212).

3) An extreme pattern where there is no resting place for the individual, even in withdrawal. He will then evolve not from

---

[1] See 'Aggression in relation to emotional development' (1950–1955) in TPTP, pp. 204–218.

the core of the self but from a shell, in which he 'exists by not being found' (TP212).

Winnicott reminds us that impingement is necessary, because the infant needs to find an object to push against. We could say that a patient sometimes needs our incorrect interpretations. He needs us to be wrong, both to indicate, as Winnicott has said, the limits of our understanding at any one time, and to facilitate his opposition to us as an object that he comes up against.

Winnicott does not argue that aggression derives from frustration. Of course, he acknowledges that there can be anger that is due to frustration, but the aggression he is addressing 'precedes the ego integration that makes anger at instinctual frustration possible, and that makes the erotic experience an experience' (TP216).

In 'The Use of an Object' he writes that he has learned to wait, not to interpret so much, in order 'to make possible . . . transference movements'(PR86). Here he is describing a particular use of the analytic object. He indicates that there are psychical states that are akin to muscle developments, that the patient grows stronger through the expression of mental states in the transference. So a patient who has been unable to express certain self states with the mother or the father is, in effect, exercising the psyche by expressing them to the analyst.

The analyst creates the opportunity for various forms of transference movement. If it is his silence that allows such movements, then the object being used is both him and not him. He is both the environment mother, because he supports the patient's right to use him, and the object mother, because he is there to be attacked by the patient. If interpretation is to be effective, it must be 'related to the patient's ability *to place the analyst outside the area of subjective phenomena*. What is then involved is the patient's ability to use the analyst' (PR87).

In other words, the analyst must not exist purely as a subjective object; he must also be an object who is objectively perceived.

Objectivity suggests survivability. The patient can now use the analyst in the precise sense that he can destroy him as an internal object, perhaps acting out against the analyst in the session, knowing that the analyst survives. Winnicott maintains that the destruction of the internal object is predicated on object relating.

Many people get confused over the idea that object relating is to be replaced by object usage. When Winnicott uses the term *object relating* in this paper, he is not talking in a general way about intimacy or human relationships. He is referring to a process that is purely subjective, involving an internal object that is created out of projections and introjections. The concept of the 'use of the object', on the other hand, takes as its focus 'the nature and the behaviour of the object.' He says, 'The object, if it is to be used must necessarily be real in the sense of being part of shared reality, not a bundle of projections' (PR88).

He reminds us of his concept of the transitional object, which is based on a paradox: the baby creates the object which is already there, waiting to be created. He writes, 'To use an object the subject must have developed a *capacity* to use objects. This is part of the change to the reality principle' (PR89). In other words, if the infant uses the actual object in a transitional way, he is already making use of the object as a thing in itself. Indeed, it is the object's thingness that allows him to destroy it, to imagine it destroyed in phantasy and then to discover its survival.

So Winnicott is saying that the infant does not have to hold the object in mind. He can destroy it now because he knows that the actual object survives the destruction of the internal object. As he discovers and rediscovers this survival, the object gradually becomes a thing in its own right, outside the subject's omnipotent control.

Moreover, because the infant comes to appreciate that the object survives his destruction, he is now free to find pleasure in destroying it. 'A new feature thus arrives in the theory of object-relating,' writes Winnicott. He continues:

The subject says to the object: 'I destroyed you', and the object is there to receive the communication. From now on the subject says: 'Hullo object!' 'I destroyed you.' 'I love you.' 'You have value for me because of your survival of my destruction of you.' (PR90)

At this point he starts to change the meaning of the use of the object. He is now saying that it is not simply the destruction of the internal object; it is also the destruction of the external object. Let's follow this idea along to its conclusion.

He is describing a new kind of experience and a different type of love. It's not the love that arrives through destruction (I eat you) but the love of the object in its own right, because of its capacity to survive. He continues, 'While I am loving you, I am all the time destroying you in unconscious phantasy.' For Winnicott, it is here that phantasy begins for the individual. The subject can now use the object that has survived.

At this point he is employing a different, less specific concept of use. When he says that the subject can now use the object, he means almost from a practical point of view, from a useful point of view. He means that destruction of the internal object continues, but the infant starts to live a life 'in the world of objects', and he stands to gain immeasurably from this.

Winnicott then takes us to his final point, presenting the most complex and interesting theory of the use of the object:

The central postulate in this thesis is that, whereas the subject does not destroy the subjective object (projection material), destruction turns up and becomes a central feature so far as the object is objectively perceived, has autonomy, and belongs to 'shared' reality. (PR91)

Here he is offering a different argument. His first theory of object use is that, through continuous destruction of the internal object and its survival, the object becomes part of the external world, and the child discovers that the object has its own integrity, its own actuality, its own personality. In his second theory of object use, there is a destruction in phantasy of the integrity of the actual object. This involves subjective object relations.

Because the adolescent knows that his phantasies, his internal constructions of the mother and the father, are not fair, he will abuse the external others. He needs to use the actual objects in this way, to destroy them, in order to create mothers and fathers in his internal world. In analysis, after the first form of object use, you then come to the second, where the patient knows the integrity of the analyst's actuality but needs to destroy him in order to give mental life to the analyst as a subjective object.

We see this when a patient feels free to say 'Oh, you always say this— well I'll tell you what I think about what you say', when in fact you haven't said a word. The patient knows that you don't actually say these things. What he is doing at that moment is imagining you in a certain way and announcing his relation to you as his subjective object. And he is doing this because he needs to do it. He has to find you as a subjective object through phantasy: a way of thinking something through internal object relations that then need to be expressed by being emptied into reality. If the patient stops and says, 'Oh, I'm really sorry. I didn't mean to say that to you', this indicates a collapse of the use of the object because he now feels guilt and is making reparation.

This is where object relating interferes with object use. When a patient can come into the room, lie down, and start talking to us about us without guilt interfering, then we are truly being made use of. This use has to do with aggression, with pleasure, and with the finding and the articulation of the object. This is why Winnicott believes that use is more important than relating, and why he believes that use is an accomplishment.

He is saying that the destructive impulse—'maximum destructiveness (object not protected)' (PR91)—comes at the moment when the infant begins to see the object as external, outside his area of omnipotence. So the destructiveness is directed towards this actual, external object, not towards an internal object. And—if things go well—the external object survives the destruction and is still there to be used.

14
Morals

We have discussed the infant's pleasure in constructing a good relation to the mother. This is a non-instinctual love, supported by the mother's pleasure in receiving it, and this mutuality is important to the effectiveness of this side of the love/hate equation.

What about guilt?

In 'The development of the capacity for concern' (1962 in DD) Winnicott establishes the following progression:

1) When the object is not destroyed it is 'because of its own survival capacity, not because of the baby's protection of the object' (DD104).

2) The infant's anxiety that he will lose the object-mother through his excited attacks on her is held in check by his contributions to the environment-mother.

3) 'Instinct-drives lead to ruthless usage of objects, and then to a guilt-sense which is held, and is allayed by the contribution to the environment-mother that the infant can make in the course of a few hours' (DD104).

4) The opportunity for making reparation enables the infant to be bolder in his experiencing of id-drives, which 'frees the baby's instinctual life' (DD 104). Good maternal care results in more confident infant destructions of the mother, without an increase in guilt.

Essential Aloneness. Christopher Bollas, Oxford University Press. © Christopher Bollas 2024.
DOI: 10.1093/oso/9780197683880.003.0014

5) 'When confidence in this benign cycle and in the expectation of opportunity is established, the sense of guilt in relation to the id-drives becomes further modified, and we then need a more positive term, such as "concern"'(DD104).

6) The infant now takes responsibility for his own instinctual impulses 'and the functions that belong to them' (DD104).

The experience of guilt is affiliated with anxiety. As Klein understood it, the infant's guilt hovers between recognition of the effects of destruction and intense fear of being attacked by the mother. But such persecutory anxiety must be borne out when the mother's management of destruction breaks down. The fear that she will retaliate, that she will do unto the infant as he has done unto her, is surely based on the experience of a mother who reacts in this way. Winnicott writes:

[F]ailure of the object-mother to survive or of the environment-mother to provide reliable opportunity for reparation leads to a loss of the capacity for concern, and to its replacement by crude anxieties and by crude defences, such as splitting, or disintegration. (DD105)

In an important essay entitled 'Morals and education' (1963), Winnicott suggests that the efforts of parents and of society to 'implant morals' (MP100) is, paradoxically, a violation of a child's innate morality. There is a natural tendency towards morality based on a child's wish 'to be like the other persons and animals who are part of the child's world' (MP100). Indeed, there are 'moral codes' that parents leave lying about in the child's world, just as they leave teddies and toys around for the child to use. 'These moral codes are given in subtle ways by expressions of acceptance or by threats of the withdrawal of love' (MP99).

Such codes are useful, but their presence is not responsible for the child's moral development. This depends on the child's use of these codes, which depends in turn on his own psycho-development. That is, children have a 'natural progress' that yields a moral development.

Winnicott cites the example of the child's control of his sphincters in bowel training. He says that there is a natural development towards sphincter control that depends not on parental pressure, but on intrinsic growth in the child. If the parent can wait, the child will generally develop his own inner morality based on his natural progress, an evolution that will leave him with a 'sense of achievement and of faith in human nature' (MP100). The experience of such innate development is very different from that produced by a parent or educator who believes that the child should be 'taught' morality.

In Winnicott's view, 'immorality for the infant is *to comply at the expense of the personal way of life*' (MP102). In other words, for the infant, a moral life is one in which his actions are derivative of the true self. A child will need time and parental patience in order to live by his own private morality, but such developments are crucial to his ultimate belief in himself.

Some parents and educators reward compliance and can mistake compliance for growth. The child can develop into a copy of a self, with true self remaining hidden.

An experience in my eight-year-old son's life comes to mind. For some two years he attended a school which seemed on the surface of things to be quite good. It was nestled in the Berkshire Mountains of New England and had lovely buildings and grounds. Unfortunately, however, the educators there were in the grip of a very particular idea that children had to be very closely marked and confronted whenever they committed a transgression.

(This sort of mentality can easily prevail in a closed community in which the elders can exercise tyrannical authority.)

One of the things I liked about my son as a boy was his boldness, even when this turned into mischief. I do not usually have difficulty telling the difference between mischievousness that reflects the ego trying things out, and destructiveness that requires firm confrontation. Knowing this, my son was generally free to be a child: in other words, he was not an adult and didn't act like one.

One day, however, there was a collision between his nature and his teacher's puritanical morality. He was playing soccer with his mates, and the ball went under a building. He offered to climb under the building to fetch it—a moment, for him, of minor heroism. His teacher saw his actions, called him to her, and told him that it was against the school rules to climb under the building. She sent him indoors, and when lessons resumed she lectured him and the class on the dangers of such exploration. Then after school she elected to tell his mother, in his presence, of his infraction.

The point of this vignette is to pose a question. If left to himself, would my son have come into his own realization of the problematics of getting the ball from under the building? Since it was a dark, damp, and dirty place, his own inner sense of good versus bad would probably have prevailed eventually, informing him internally that this was not a good place to be. Furthermore, he had gone in there in order to retrieve a ball, not because he was looking for a rebellious independent adventure. And it had involved no danger: he would be able to distinguish between climbing under a building and running across a street.

Had this teacher wanted to impress upon him a rule whilst at the same time supporting his own inner sense of right and wrong (based on ego capacities), she might have said 'Pretty filthy place, eh?' This would have affirmed his own experience and perception as well as her role in noting its 'off-limits' status. Were he to do it again, as a matter of independent desire, then she might tell him that he should not have been there.

In 'Aggression and its roots' (1939), Winnicott argues that by giving the infant time to develop, the mother enables him to be destructive, to be able to hate. This the infant achieves by actual kicking and screaming instead of magically annihilating the world. He writes:

In this way *actual aggression is seen to be an achievement.* As compared with magical destruction, aggressive ideas and behaviour take on a positive value, and hate becomes a sign of civilization, when we keep in mind the whole process of the emotional development of the individual, and especially the earliest stages. (DD 98–9).

How different is this view of civilization from Freud's? In *Civilisation and Its Discontents*, Freud argues that it is guilt driven by the superego—that is the price of civilization. I think this view is correct, or at least it is a plausible myth that is psychologically accurate in terms of the oedipal period, when guilt deriving from murderous wishes is an important factor in the creation of a society.

However, Winnicott's thinking applies to an earlier period, to infancy, when the mother allows the infant to bring his hate into the world of actual objects and to discover that they both survive this. Such maternal provision enables the infant to transform a psychic force into an experience: to put a mental state into the object world. Relief is to be had via this externalizing, and the need to be able to hate recognizes the civilizing function of living from the true self. By feeling real and operating from inside his own psyche-soma, the infant will eventually be able to develop concern for the object based on the freedom of his own beliefs, rather than being governed by premature compliance and reactive living.

One of the most eloquent and moving articles written by Winnicott was given as a talk on the radio in 1945. Entitled 'Home Again', it addressed parents who were waiting for the return of their children who had been evacuated from the city to the countryside during the War. What he said will serve both as a preface to our consideration of his view of the deprived child and as a point of embarkation for our subsequent discussion on play.

In 'Home Again'[1] he said:

---

[1] In DD, pp. 49–53.

Here are the children home again, filling our ears with sounds that had long been almost dead. People had forgotten that children are noisy creatures, but now they are being reminded. Schools are reopening. . . Back streets have become cricket pitches, with the children gradually adapting themselves to town traffic. Round the street corners come bands of Nazis or other kinds of gangsters, complete with guns improvised out of sticks, hunters and hunted alike oblivious of the passer-by. (DD49)

At the centre of the child's universe is the home. 'When he is home', Winnicott writes, 'he really knows what home is like, and because of this he is free to pretend it is anything he wants it to be for the purposes of his play' (DD50). The home is an extension and developmental displacement of the maternal holding environment. It is the area of security, of known reliability that supports the child's freedom. 'Play is not just pleasure—it is essential to his well-being' (DD50), and it is the home that provides the basis for the capacity to play.

In 'The absence of a sense of guilt' (1966), Winnicott describes a pattern in which an 'antisocial tendency' emerges. It is worth bearing in mind that such a tendency can be a normal part of an ordinary child's life. A child who wets his bed, for example, expresses this antisocial tendency in that this act breaks up the family peace of mind.

There is a stage before 'the arrival of secondary gains' which displays one of the features of delinquent life. It is when 'the child needs help and feels mad because of being compelled from within to steal, to destroy' (DD110). Such a feeling of madness can only be relieved by acting it out so as to announce to the world that madness is present and needs attending to.

Winnicott maintains that when a child is disturbed beyond his ego capacities he will become hopeful by committing antisocial acts that compel society to 'go back with him or her to the position where things went wrong, and to acknowledge the fact' (DD110).

A child may steal from the local shop, and this small crime may force the parents to take the child for a psychotherapy consultation, or perhaps, if they are insightful parents, it will encourage them to consult with themselves. In a good situation the parents and the child come to understand where things have broken down in the child's life.

'Then the child can reach back to the period before the moment of deprivation', writes Winnicott, and 'rediscover the good object and the good human controlling environment which by existing originally enabled him or her to experience impulses, including destructive ones' (DD110–11). If this is successful, the child should no longer be driven to act out. His stealing invited attention, but it also risked incurring moral censure. If he were then to be defined as a criminal, he would be deprived of the opportunity for healthy destructiveness.

Winnicott claims in 1946 that when a child steals outside his home he is 'still looking for the mother'[2] (DD116). However, this search indicates an agitation and frustration that also reflects a need for a 'paternal authority that can and will put a limit to the actual effect of his impulsive behaviour' (DD116). In what he calls 'full blown delinquency', the child is in acute need for a 'strict father who will protect mother when she is found' (DD116). Only when he finds this strong father can the child regain control of his loving impulses, feel guilt, and 'wish to mend' (DD116).

The delinquent has a need to get into trouble. By being a nuisance he compels the community to attend to him, but this does not necessarily restrict his capacity to love. Indeed, antisocial acts may be a means of preserving his love of the parents. If the child cannot create a nuisance when he needs to, then he will become inhibited in his love, depressed and depersonalized. Eventually he will be 'unable to feel the reality of things at all, except the reality of violence' (DD116).

[2] See 'Some psychological aspects of juvenile delinquency' (1946) in DD, pp.113–119.

According to Winnicott, it is generally the passing of time that cures the adolescent of the phase-specific illness that afflicts him. Each adolescent is essentially an isolate who is always on the verge of a depression. Adolescents come together and will tend to identify with singularly disturbed members of the group—such as those who commit suicide, steal, or take drugs—because such individual acts represent states of mind that exist within each of them.

Central to Winnicott's vision of the adolescent is the analyst's responsibility to tolerate aggression and actings-out as indications of hope, of faith in the right to a personal creation of reality. The adolescent begins by seeming to destroy his objects—including the parents—but such destruction in fact expresses a form of creativity as he tries to rise, phoenix-like, out of the ashes of his destruction.

This is the second period in a person's life when the environment is attacked in a manner that aims to reintroduce the principles of use of the object. The adolescent needs to destroy parents as childhood objects in order to find the adult in them. To do so requires a kind of manic triumph over the parental ideal. Since the child holds an idealized inner parent inside him, he must shatter this in order to accept the real parent—imperfections and all.

Perhaps he needs to be emboldened by manic affect, as the effect of the loss of his childhood parents is quite devastating. Unlike the small child, he is distressed by the disturbing realization that he could inflict actual damage. The severely disturbed adolescent can actually kill the parents, and certainly he can damage them emotionally in a way that was impossible only a few years earlier.

At this stage it can be very difficult for parents to identify with their parenting function when their ideals linked to this function are being trampled on by the adolescent. In this respect, parents and child must now find ways to survive the mutual loss of ideals: the child's loss of ideal parents, the parents' loss of the ideal child.

15

Playing and Creativity

In his extraordinary and deceptively simple paper 'Playing: a theoretical statement', Winnicott says that 'psychotherapy takes place in
the overlap of two areas of playing, that of the patient and that of the
therapist' (PR38).

In order to understand why he puts complex ideas in such simple
terms, we need to bear in mind the context in which he lived. He
had a deep appreciation for the genius of Melanie Klein, and no
doubt he was able to point out where and how her interpretations
constituted an act of play. For example, in reviewing her work with
Dick, it is possible to see how the child brought his inner world into
sessions and how his play overlapped with Klein's own playing, in
the form of her use of her newfound ideas. In this respect, Klein
played with Dick through her interpretations; as Dick played with
his toys, Klein played with her ideas.

Winnicott cites Milner's statement that children's playing and
adult analysand's concentration may not be merely a defensive regression, but 'an essential recurrent phase of a creative relation to
the world'[1] (PR38). He claims that we must look at playing not just
in terms of its content, but as a thing-in-itself. It seems to me that
psychoanalysts have used play to derive meanings, but they have
not looked carefully enough at playing as a process.

Playing takes place initially in a potential space between the infant and the mother. It is an action in the transitional space between
the purely internal and the actual. The transitional object is the first

---

[1] Winnicott cites Milner, 'Aspects of symbolism in comprehension of the not-self',
International Journal of Psychoanalysis volume 33. 1952.

Essential Aloneness. Christopher Bollas, Oxford University Press. © Christopher Bollas 2024.
DOI: 10.1093/oso/9780197683880.003.0015

plaything, and the spirit of play is authorized by maternal provision. Through her management of the infant's needs and setting, the mother sustains a holding environment that enables the infant to live from a relaxed, non-reactive kernel of self.

From this subjective place the true self brings its inherited potential into moments of being through object use. As the infant commits himself to such creativity, the mother continues to facilitate his use of objects by bringing them into his view or grasp. For the first few months she presents objects in this somewhat magical way, providing the infant with an experience of omnipotence. The repetition of these facilitations enables him to fuse aggressive and libidinal cathexes of objects, and it is essential to his growing sense that he can live from the core of the self.

At some point the infant becomes aware of this precise facilitation on the mother's part. Then, when he plays, he creates an illusion of omnipotence that allows for his creation of characters and plot (teddy and doggy go looking for mummy). In this way the child discovers the uses of illusion, as this cultural inheritance is transmitted through play and relating. The creative rights of the self depend on the inscription of such freedom by the mother. Winnicott writes:

> Play is immensely exciting. It is exciting, *not primarily because the instincts are involved,* be it understood! The thing about playing is always the precariousness of the interplay of personal psychic reality and the experience of control of actual objects. (PR47)

Such precariousness exists because there is an inevitable tension present in the moment when a child or adult wonders if play is possible. We all recall, no doubt, our question to friends in latency: 'Want to come and play?' or to the parents: 'Can Mike come out to play now?' Or, later, that moment when we say to a friend, 'Would you like to go to the Gilel's concert next week?' or 'Have you heard the joke about the two psychoanalysts who grew up together?'

We can never be entirely sure that our wish to play will be reciprocated. Indeed, if play were an unconditional right, its terms easily met (like eating or breathing), then some of the excitement that is intrinsic to the joys of play would be absent.

At the heart of playing is a question, one that is only ever expressed as a derivative such as 'Do you want to play?' The underlying question asks, 'Is play possible? Do we have the right to play at this moment?' Thus in the moments just before the initiation of playing, the question inevitably arises as to whether play can be present or not. And one of the reasons playing is joyful is that it provides the answer. Playing is its own celebration, and the products of play, even when they are great works of art, are always less significant than the fact that playing was possible.

Could it be that Winnicott turned to a concept of play because the same problematic inherent in the question of play—to play or not to play—was at stake in the field of psychoanalysis? Was psychoanalysis to be taken over by theological fanatics who transformed its truths into catholicized habits of thought? Or might its discoveries remain as tentative objects, available for use in any particular moment between patient and analyst? His thinking suggests that the use of a psychoanalytical object depends on the rights of play. Is this right present, or not? Is the law of the mother in effect?

'When a patient cannot play', wrote Winnicott, 'the therapist must attend to this major symptom before interpreting fragments of behaviour' (PR47). Such an attendance is not so easy. Indeed, years may go by before playing becomes a possibility, in which case a period of 'standard analysis' of the patient's anxieties, depressions, and their transference manifestations may be essential.

The idea that playing is an aim within an analysis relates to the drive for freedom in any oppressed person. However, the psychoanalyst's enabling of his patient's freedom is not the same process as escaping from an oppressive regime. Within the individual patient there is no such clear boundary between areas of oppression and freedom. Instead the analyst strives, with a turn of phrase, or through humour, to enable a moment's play with the analysand in an effort to establish this as a rightful human experience.

It is clear that Winnicott thought such a right was not present in 'Kleinianism', although it was there in the practice of Melanie Klein herself. It is always an element in the creative discoveries of a gifted analyst, but all too often it can be missing in that person's adherents, who can become attached like glue to the ideas of a creator. Lacan clearly enjoyed his mischievous brilliance and was at play, but this was a quality strikingly absent, for the most part, in the legions of acolytes who have followed him and who speak for his name.

Winnicott sought to stand up for this right, not simply by calling for its recognition but by embodying the principles of play in his manner of representing the argument. He was an impish person, an individual endowed with a natural playfulness.

He was reluctant to allow the word 'creativity' to be appropriated by the artistic world. He believed that ordinary people are creative if they approach life in a creative way. The 'creative impulse' is therefore something that can be looked at as a thing in itself (PR69).[2] While it is a necessary precursor to an artist's production, it is equally present 'when *anyone*—baby, child, adolescent, adult, old man or woman—looks in a healthy way at anything or does anything deliberately' (PR69).

In his essay 'Creativity and its origins', Winnicott says that to analyse a creative artist's work in relation to their sexuality—for example Freud's effort to link Leonardo da Vinci's work to his homosexuality—is irritating, and for good reason. It is because it looks as if we are getting somewhere when in fact 'the direction of inquiry is wrong' (PR69). 'The main theme', he says, 'is being

---

[2] See 'Creativity and its origins', PR, pp. 65–85.

circumvented, that of the creative impulse itself. The creation stands between the observer and the artist's creativity' (PR69).

With regard to Freudian and Kleinian theories of creativity, Winnicott claims that the concept of the primacy of the death instinct constitutes a refusal to look at the 'full implication of dependence and therefore of the environmental factor' (PR70–1). The death instinct is 'a reassertion of the principle of original sin' (PR70). He continues, '. . . the history of an individual baby cannot be written in terms of the baby alone. It must be written in terms also of the environmental provision which either meets dependence needs or fails to meet them' (PR71).

By discarding the primacy of the death instinct, and of the hereditary factor in determining the balance of death versus life, Winnicott places personal creativity at the very heart of the individual. If maternal care is good enough, if the mother helps the baby to survive the shock of the loss of omnipotence, then the baby can gradually relate internal, subjective objects to objects objectively perceived.

Because objects then feel as if they derive from deep subjectivity, this transfer of cathexes enables him to feel real and to have a creative relation to the outside world. Klein's object world is overly malevolent, whereas Winnicott's objects bear the reassuring imprint of the creative form of life. The infant somehow knows that the objects he creates are his, and the chaotic disposition of the paranoid-schizoid position becomes real only when a breakdown occurs in the holding environment.

In Lacanian theory, the baby feels that through the object he finds the other's image of himself, thereby splitting the subject into an imaginary and a symbolic order. I do think this split is meaningful, but it is presented as more anguishing than it needs to be, as Lacan does not consider the infant's creative relation to reality, specifically the ability to endow objects with subjective life.

Nothing, in my view, gives us a clearer glimpse into Winnicott's own personal creativity then his paper on this very subject.

However, some readers are puzzled by his sudden turn to an entirely new topic, the masculine and the feminine, which he links only fleetingly and tangentially to his theory of creativity.

He describes a session with a male patient who had had twenty-five years of analysis without getting to the factor that was eventually crucial to his potential change. He writes:

> In the present phase of this analysis something has been reached which is new *for me*. It has to do with the way I am dealing with the non-masculine element in his personality. (PR73)

Taking full responsibility for his leap in theory, he tells his patient: 'I am listening to a girl. I know perfectly well that you are a man but I am listening to a girl, and I am talking to a girl. I am telling this girl: "you are talking about penis envy"' (PR73).

The patient was deeply moved by this comment, but Winnicott felt he should go further. He continues:

> It was my next remark that surprised me and it clinched the matter. I said: 'It was not that *you* told this to anyone; it is *I* who see the girl and hear a girl talking, when actually there is a man on my couch. The mad person is *myself.* (PR73–4)

This creative moment allowed the patient to feel sane in a mad environment. 'For my part', writes Winnicott, 'I have needed to live through a deep personal experience in order to arrive at the understanding I feel I now have reached' (PR74).

From this personal discovery Winnicott is eventually able to show the patient how the patient's mother saw him as a girl when in fact he was a boy. Looking back, he says that the second part of his interpretation was something he nearly did not allow himself to make.

Yet we had here something new, new in my own attitude and new in his capacity to make use of my interpretive work. I decided to surrender myself to whatever this might mean in myself, and the result is to be found in this paper that I am presenting. (PR75)

I know of no clearer representation of creative work in analysis than this episode recorded by Winnicott. It epitomizes his inner freedom and his capacity to entertain a new idea which processes his private experiencing of the analysand.

Elsewhere I have said that I think contemporary psychoanalysts have not sufficiently utilized a self-analytical element. This is equivalent to the parent's capacity for self-reflection, but it also requires a capacity in the analyst for inner play. This is its own inspiration, and through it new ideas will emerge in a certain spirit of offering hypothetical ideas rather than declaring truths.

Winnicott was surprised by his perception of the patient's penis envy. He surrendered to an as yet unthought known experience, and then, through an additional surprising remark, he suddenly knows what he thinks. As he has embodied the spirit of self-analysis, he has conveyed this to his patient, and a spirit of play is established.

It is meaningless, it seems to me, to separate form and content at such a point. It is immaterial whether it is the precise idea (content) or its arrival in a certain spirit (form) that is transformative, because the idea and the spirit of creation are inseparable. But it is possible to claim that only through his surrender to the unthought known could Winnicott emerge with an inspired idea.

And certainly his manner of using the psychoanalytical space will have conveyed itself to the analysand, who was licensed by example to surrender to an imaginative act that could work on the unthought known. Such surrender and its resultant inspiration is the stuff of creativity and of life.

16

Questions

Q: *What happens to the male element in the girl as she enters the Oedipus complex?*

A: With the hysteric, the male element in the mother-child relation is ultimately transferable to the oedipal situation. If the mother has the father and the male element within her and in her mothering, if she can represent the male element to the infant, it helps pave the way to a good enough oedipal situation.

Q: *We develop both instinctually and as selves. How do we coordinate these two tracks?*

A: I think there is an interweaving of instinctual life and the evolution of being that Winnicott defines as the axis of the development of self. In discussing the marriage of instinctual and self evolution, we consider two vectors crucial to psychoanalytical theory. The first is the one that Freud assigns to fulfil the discharge function of instinctual tensions. This can be an ideational object—an idea of the object allows the instinct to be fulfilled.

Winnicott focuses on the second object, the one that is there in external reality as the psyche-soma of the mother or father. For example, let's say that the instinctual derivative emerges as thirst. Soon, the mother presents the breast and the baby drinks. At that moment the two objects link. It is the mother's organization of the dialectic between the two objects that, in my view, coordinates the mutual evolution of instinct and self.

Q: *In what way does a child achieve health through the function of illusion? And how do we use illusion to contact reality?*

Essential Aloneness. Christopher Bollas, Oxford University Press. © Christopher Bollas 2024.
DOI: 10.1093/oso/9780197683880.003.0016

A: I think the answer lies in the particular function of an illusion that creates an experience of omnipotence. The mother sustains an illusion that the infant creates the world and, ironically, it is this illusion that permits him to gather together the details of reality. The objects of reality seem to emerge from the wishes and needs of the infant.

Q: *What is the role of disillusionment in terms of the decline of omnipotence?*

A: For Winnicott, disillusionment is an incremental activity managed by the mother, as she gradually informs the infant of the objective nature of reality. I think we can add to this that the infant also discovers the objectivity of life in its own right, when he finds that his objects do not correspond to his wishes. So psycho-development is in itself a procedure, a means of working towards health. Once the infant can reach for an object by himself, without the mother's facilitation, he discovers that sometimes the object falls out of his hand. This is an instructive frustration because it helps him learn things about the world.

We know the surprise the baby has when he bumps into an object. It is not so much that he is hurt or in pain—he is in a state of disbelief! How could this happen? And of course when the walking child repeatedly falls down and gets up again, the entire experience is curative of the illusion of omnipotence.

So from Winnicott's point of view, psycho-development is curative. He places great emphasis on the maturational process, on a natural evolution towards health that will take place in the person if the conditions are favourable. And later on we shall see how this idea figures in his theory of psychoanalytical practice.

Q: *Do you think that in some ways it is normal for a mother to experience a depression after giving birth?*

A: Yes, I think it is ordinary for a mother to experience a postpartum depression of one kind or another. For every woman there must be an unconscious memory of the loss of total environmental provision, because this was true of the loss of her own intrauterine existence. This is why it is so important for breast feeding to be mutually pleasurable, because libido—the pleasure of instinctual mutuality—is a recuperative factor.

Q: *Can you say more about the transition from aloneness to dependency?*

A: From Winnicott's point of view there is a state of double dependency during aloneness. The foetus is dependent upon the intrauterine state, and the mother is also dependent upon the foetus. This is a dependence of which the foetus has no knowledge, so Winnicott discriminates between dependence that is not known about and dependence that is consciously experienced. He believes that in the weeks just before birth there is a dawning of awareness of the environment, but he distinguishes this from the infant's recognition of the mother, which, obviously, comes much later.

Q: *What type of aloneness are we considering? Does it precede dependence?*

A: This is what Winnicott calls a paradox. You are right that he said it comes before dependence. Later he says that of course dependence is there in the womb, but the foetus has no knowledge of it. So is it possible that he is still trying to work through in his mind what this primary aloneness actually is? I think the aloneness that he is describing is that state of being that exists soon after the emergence from inorganic to organic life (i.e. from non-existence to existence), when there is, we assume, minimal registration of stimuli either from the inside (soma or psyche) or the outside (external world).

Q: *How do you think of dreams and fantasy in terms of serving the true self?*

A: There are some dreams and fantasies that do not simply represent instinctual derivatives, but objectify the movements of the true self. And some of our relationships in life reflect our own evolution. For example, when we fall in love, we are absolutely sure of the choice. We do not question it. It just happens. But how can we explain why we fall in love with this particular person? Our choice of love object has to do with the unconscious elaboration of our intrinsic design. Something is there in this other that evokes our idiom and there is a match.

We can't explain these specific choices, but they are often realizations of our true self. They have a decisiveness, a clarity, an assuredness that is beyond reflective thinking. It is as if we find an object (a person, a book, a composer) through which the true self can move, so we can elaborate and fulfil ourselves. If I read Melville, I can find my way through the fiction and have many reflections. This is my choice and I can move through the object.

We never just read the text. The text reads us. It creates room for us to move. Long ago, when I first read Jane Austen, I seemed to come up against a wall. It was just not my object and I felt stuck. I could only suffer her. For me it was a purely academic issue of having to read the book so as to be able to understand Jane Austen. This would change over time as I struggled with her fiction, a necessary part of the dialectics of experience.

Q: *You said some time ago that you did not like Mahler's music when you first heard it. So your true self was unable to engage with it?*

A: Often it is important that we struggle with an object, that we negotiate something between our own internal aims, wishes and idioms, and the specific aesthetic organization of the object. And there is much to learn about the negotiation of difficulty. After the dialectic of resistance and attraction, are we able to move, as it were, through the object towards elaboration of our own self experience?

Q: *If we do not manage to realize our true self, do we grieve this loss? Does it precipitate a depression?*

A: At first this might be seen as a form of depression, but I think this is not the right term. It is more like a held sadness, a body monument that commemorates the death of an aspect of the true self. My concept of the unthought known includes the idea that we have some inner knowledge that enables us, potentially, to recognize and allow grief over the loss of the unlived self.

When, for example, a divorce occurs and a new partner is found, there can be an intense, joyful movement and creativity as we realize parts of the self that had never been lived before. There are some marriages in which the choice of a partner is a bad choice. Perhaps it was a way of recreating an original obstruction to the realization of true self, often obstructions that were in the mother and father.

A person's choice of partner can bring us to a diagnostic moment. Adolescents will often be attracted to someone who is fragile or vulnerable, but anytime you hear the statement 'But I love him because he needs me'—watch out! Ultimately this choice will involve a closing down of the true self in order to fulfil the needs of the other, and in fact this is the person's own need projected into the partner. The transformation is equivalent to the original loss: infant needs mother, but if mother's need for the infant is greater, then the legitimate needs of infant can become lost.

Q: *What exactly do you mean when you talk about celebrating the child?*

A: We should let the child know that we are interested in the facts of his instinctual life. Rather than trying to interpret the unconscious meaning of a communication, this can often be done more effectively by showing surprise, or by celebrating his affects. We all know from our experience of working with children that our insightful interpretations about how babies get inside mummy's tummy will often evoke a simple 'No'!

In the case we have been hearing about, the analyst celebrates her patient when he opens the truck. She says 'Ah, secrets!', and in response to the robot, 'Ah, what a big robot!' The aim here is to celebrate the symbolic representation of the child's body self, and to link this representation with the object relation in the transference. I think an analysis needs to proceed as a dialectic of celebration and interpretation.

Q: *Might you be celebrating 'the maturational process'?*

A: I agree. There are developmental paradigms which need celebration within the analysis. At different phases of separation in life, it is important for the analyst to welcome the patient's aggression against the analyst.

I once wrote an ironic postcard to a psychotic adolescent patient. I knew that it was important to him to pretend that my absence was of no significance. His response to my departure was, 'Ah, two weeks! Now I can do what I want!' So I wrote: 'I know that you are dying without me!'

In a way I was celebrating the independence of self. I believe it is wrong to insist, again and again, 'No, I really think you are going to miss me', as if we want to implant a piece of psychoanalytical ideology into the patient. When a patient misses the analyst this is a very important moment, very delicate, very sophisticated. To miss the analyst is a form of object relating: he is missing the analyst as other.

Q: *Do you think your concept of celebration of the analysand derives from your training in the Independent Group in England?*

A: I'm grateful to my own analysts in London who did celebrate their patients. In particular, however, I owe much to Marion Milner who always celebrated the patient.

I think of a manic-depressive patient (discussed earlier) who would tell me in each session that he wanted to kill me. He meant this in a certain kind of way: he really meant that he did not want me to say anything. However, I would interpret to him what he was doing, giving fairly common analytical interpretations about his omnipotence, his annihilation of the object and so on.

He was a very bright and intelligent man. One day his annihilation of an interpretation that I had made was rather extraordinary. It amused me, even though I was the object of considerable verbal destruction. So I said to him, 'My God . . . bravo!' At the end of the session I asked, 'Well, do you think I'm going to be able to get up out of my chair to see you to the door?'

This moment changed the atmosphere of the analysis. From then on when he was being destructive, I would say, 'Ah, so it's kill Bollas day.'

Because he was so ill, psychoanalytical interpretation felt like an assault. Interpretation can become a kind of counter-murder, equivalent to taking the patient to pieces. We have to find an alternative to this so that psychoanalysis is not a counterforce, like a slap back. We need, instead, to celebrate the analysand's mental giftedness, even when it is used to destroy us.

I did not know Winnicott but I knew his wife, Clare, and Martin James, Enid Balint, Nina Coltart, and other people in the Independent group. I think one of their great contributions to psychoanalysis has been their way of discovering the positive elements amidst the most destructive formations. Amongst the most destructive fantasies and behaviour, they could find the child's effort to create a solution to an impossible situation. And it is this capacity to discover the positive aim—we could say the life instincts—that I believe differentiates their work from the Kleinian thinking of that time.

Q: *What is the effect on the analysis of repetition in a child's play?*

A: What an interesting question. Let me start with music. In a way, receiving material that is repeated is like listening to a piece of music again and again. Part of the function of repetition in music is that the experience is never the same twice. Even though we may know the work very well, our inner response will never be identical to our previous hearings. Each time we discover elements that have not struck us before. And I am sure that the function of listening in analysis is not dissimilar.

Perhaps this is what is meant by the working through process. The emphasis has traditionally been on the idea that there must be a long period in which the patient works through his resistances. But in this context I believe that working through has more to do with the different self states that the patient is in at each moment of hearing the interpretation. It may take a long time for the total personality to have taken it in. So this has less to do with resistance than the need for time.

Q: *How does your theory of the unthought known fit in here?*

A: Originally I intended this term to refer to what the infant knows, partly through inherited knowledge, and partly through operational paradigmatic transactions with the mother. It is an operational logic that has not been thought representationally. That is, it has not achieved the form of fantasy or of abstract thinking, so we cannot use the word 'thought' as we would ordinarily understand it.

The other area in which I now use this concept is the child's storing of self experiences that are beyond comprehension. To begin with, these are experiences of life within the family. They constitute the child's ambiance. He lives in a climate and he knows it but cannot think it, so it is beyond understanding. This type of unthought known is different from the unthought known of operational transactions.

Fundamentally, from a theoretical point of view, I am trying to address mental phenomena that are known about but that have not been repressed. In other words, in a topographical theory of the mind, we cannot say that these phenomena are dynamically unconscious. We can only say they are unconscious in the sense in which the unconscious ego organizes experience.

Q: *Could you say more about your interest in the evocative dimensions in analysis?*

A: The word 'evocation', as you know, comes from *evocare* which means 'to call forth'. The word 'celebration' also means 'to call to the ceremony'. I think this has something to do with the analyst's creation of an atmosphere that is conducive to the kind of object relating that facilitates true self activity. If this atmosphere is not created in the analysis, then in my view true self will not be present.

One of the great Freudian concepts, and the core feature of a Lacanian psychoanalysis, is the idea that we do not know what we think until we speak. That is, the subject is revealed through his speech. So in the course of free association the unconscious speaks the subject, and it is only through this freedom that the subject discovers what he truly thinks.

One of Winnicott's great discoveries is that we do not know our own being except through experiencing. Thus we can say that the analysand does not know the idiom of his particular true self except through his conscious and unconscious experiencing inside the analysis.

There are innumerable elements of personality, and they all have a different function that will articulate, through being, the elements of the inherited disposition. Winnicott terms this particular process 'personalization', the development (or filling in) for each individual of his own unique character.

But often we have patients in analysis who have not been able to articulate their being through experiencing in their families. They may have developed a false self, or they may have bailed into psychotic states, prevented from coming into being. In these situations, a central task of psychoanalysis will be to facilitate the emergence of this person's true self.

Q: *How can we understand this?*

A: Let me use the language of object relations theory to differentiate between a being state and a self state. In the course of the analysis a patient could bring into the transference a particular idea that proves upon reflection to be a maternal introject: a feature of the other. This introject is part of the individual's state of being at that moment, but it is not strictly speaking a self state. We could term it an unconscious representation of the other. So in the course of an analysis, amongst other things, a patient discovers what is true of him and for him, and what is true of the other.

Some internal objects are endopsychic object representations, something not taken in from the outside but created fundamentally from the inside, from the unthought known. The more I work on Winnicott's thinking, the more the concept of the true self becomes crucial to working with his theory.

When a small child sees the shadow from his toy rocket on the wall at bedtime, he may play with the image of that rocket. He may pilot it to Mars and explore the heavens, but now and then he may just gaze at the shadow it casts on the wall, scrutinizing the relation between the real rocket and its shadow. When he uses the rocket's shadow to pilot a craft into outer space, he does so knowing that this is make-believe.

So although we call this the space of illusion, we are using the spatial metaphor to designate a capacity: the ability to 'make believe'. This English phrase may suggest that this is an intended construction, but the child resting in his bed at night, gazing at his room and finding the shadow of the rocket, has not planned to create a daydream of rocketing off into space. Furthermore, he does not know at the point of this discovery what will be made out of this illusion. The unpredictability of the use of illusion is as crucial to what emerges as the unpredictability of speech to Freud. What free association is to the Freudian, the use of illusion is to the Winnicottian.

Within the capacity to use illusion, true self shows up. It arrives through spontaneous play with an object under special conditions.

Q: *Is the transitional object a part object?*

A: We can say that the transitional object is a part object in the sense that it represents a vast unending process. However, in the Kleinian sense of the term, which refers specifically to an internal object, it is not a part object.

The concept of the transitionality of an object is determined by the infant's use of it. A teddy bear is not in itself a transitional object; it is only transitional if the infant uses it transitionally.

The internal function of a part object from the Kleinian point of view is not equivalent to the transitional object as a part object in the Winnicottian sense. He is also careful to discuss the fate of the transitional object. What happens after the use of the transitional object, and what is its subsequent status? Does it become internalized and hence can we refer to it as an internal object?

He says not, as over time its transitional function is forgotten and its use abandoned. Instead, innumerable other objects are found and used. The transitional object does not undergo repression; the person finds its counterpart in the internal world as the inner experience of the transitional process. It is not an object representation. It is the inner trace of a type of creativity. The infant's use of transitional objects enlivens the internal object world.

Q: *What is the function of the father in the child's relation to the transitional object?*

A: Winnicott answers this quite specifically. He argues that the function of the father is to support the mother so that she in turn can maintain the holding environment.

By support he does not mean that the father simply goes out and buys the groceries or does the laundry. The father's most crucial support is to realize the partnership of the male. He has to preserve alive in the mother her relation to her father and to her own male element. One example of the male element would be the capacity of the mother to put the baby down and walk away. In other words, to move out of the primary maternal role.

Another derivative of the male element is the relation to, and cathexis of, the outside world. So if there is a deficiency in the maintenance of the male element in the nursing couple, there will be a kind of collapse as mother, father, and baby go into and stay inside a very regressed situation.

There is a form of paternal holding environment that has something to do with a very special relationship that a father makes with a baby. This is partly a function of his particular intrinsic characteristics, which are very familiar to the infant, who knows what it is to be held by the father just as much as he knows what it is to be held by the mother. Unlike the mother, the father cannot assume his identity and role for the infant, so this paternal holding environment also has something to do with the way in which he presents himself to the baby as an object. Over time, one of his tasks is to represent the laws of social existence. Lacan has written a great deal about this.

Q: *Do you think there is a difference between the infant's use of his tongue or thumb and the role of the first transitional object? I'm thinking here about Gaddini's idea of the 'precursor object'.*

A: This raises an important question: what drives a human being to form this kind of object?

The thumb or the tongue is not an external object, nor is it an identification with the mother. We could say that it is precursive, in that when the infant uses the body as object of play, it is a precursor to playing with an actual external thing. Of course, there is a development from the baby's use of his own body to the use of other objects, and we can see a transition from precursor object to transitional object.

Q: *Are we talking about how the baby makes reality?*

A: Yes. In Winnicott's scheme, the infant does not discover reality, he makes it. The transitional object is the means through which the infant creates his world. If the transitional object is being used defensively because of persecutory anxiety, then we would have to see it as a misuse of the transitional object. This would show itself in perhaps an overuse of the transitional object, a repetitive and anxious overuse of it.

This making actual is a crucial contribution on the mother's part. At first she gives the baby what he needs from herself, then she gives him what he needs from the object world, thus extending the baby's range of subjectivity.

In the Kleinian theory of symbol formation, the infant creates new objects because the anxiety associated with the primary object (the mother's breast) is so intense. It drives the infant to form substitutes in order to symbolically articulate the anxieties of being with the mother. In Winnicott's scheme, on the other hand, the evolution of subjectivity and symbolization is a facilitation by the mother when she presents the infant with objects that give him pleasure. Here the evolution of the symbolic arrives through pleasure, not through anxiety.

In fact the two views are not mutually exclusive. There are certain people who are very disturbed, and we could say their symbolic formations are the result of the sort of anxieties that Klein speaks of. However, there are others for whom the symbolic formations would correspond more to Winnicott's theory of symbol formation.

There are probably many different elements in the total phenomenon that we call creativity. It seems to me likely that in each creative person one element comes from the pleasurable use of the transitional objects, and another comes from anxiety and the need to symbolically represent that particular psychic state.

To go back to Winnicott and the making actual of subjectivity: in doing this I think the baby unconsciously identifies with the mother's creativity. To some extent the infant's use of the transitional object will be in the nature of an interpretation by the infant of the mother's creative adaptation to him.

Q: *If it is the case that the infant's use of the transitional object is an act of identification with the mother, would this not substantially structure and limit his freedom? Might it, indeed, be a form of defence?*

A: When I used the word identification, I did not mean identification as a defensive activity. I meant it at a tactile, kinesthetic, sensory level—a sensory level at which somatic pleasure is linked up to an object and extended symbolically. It starts with the soma. It is extended by the proximity of an object, and soma achieves a new pleasure through the use of the object. Therefore, when the infant grasps his transitional object, he does so after many experiences of the mother presenting the breast, cleaning the body, clothing the body, presenting all kinds of objects—cuddly animals, mobiles, images, soft toys with her smell. These experiences are not identifications with the psychology of the mother; they are identifications within the sensorium.

So in a certain kind of way, the transitional object is the first vocabulary for the infant. As a vocabulary, it can be used to make many statements. At each moment the infant will be commenting on his state of being through use of the transitional object.

About this time the infant is beginning to have a sense of the future, of a tomorrow. This is possible because he has started to be able to differentiate between right now, two hours ago, and yesterday. When he develops a transitional object, he believes that the object will still be around tomorrow, and he can therefore invest it with a large quantity of libido. If he does not find it in the present, he senses that it must still be there; he asks where is it, and he looks for it.

In some ways a transitional object is a symbolic representation of ontogenesis. It is as if the infant has grasped the ingredients of what it is to be human—to make actual our own subjectivity and to communicate it. So the transitional object is also memory because it stores the past. It is utility because it is made use of in the present. And it is vision because it is connected with the future. All these complex phenomena that make up much of what it is to be human are becoming established by the infant in his use of the transitional object.

Q: *Is the transitional object a symbol?*

A: Whether it is a piece of blanket or a teddy bear, the transitional object is not itself a symbol; it is the process through which symbols are created. Its significance lies in its use as a means of articulating and elaborating the true self. When an infant projects something into it so that it is used as a symbol, it then has a static representational meaning. There may be a foreclosure. We would then very likely be talking about either a fetish or a perverse object that is no longer fulfilling multifaceted experiences.

To go on a bit, in the 1950s and 1960s, psychoanalysts inspired by Winnicott's idea came up with many different ways of talking about the transitional object. Transitional object as fetish. Transitional object as perversion. Transitional object as ossified anxiety. Transitional object as breast. Transitional object as foot. Transitional object as earth. Transitional object as . . . well, it just went on and on and on. So I think it's important to forget the object, and look at the quality of experience in the transitional space.

Q: *What is the difference between mind and psyche in Winnicott's theory?*

A: This is a clinical distinction. It allows us to distinguish patients who simply report ideas that come to mind, from those whose report is not simply a cognitive account but is infused with layered emotional psychic textures. A report from the analysand's psyche creates an intermediate space for both participants; it elicits the analyst's psychic response to the analysand rather than simply existing as a cognitive moment.

So depending upon the capacity of mind—it might provide creative facilitation or intellectualized obstructiveness—psyche may or may not be adequately represented.

In short, psyche refers to the character and characters of our 'internal world', whilst mind refers to our mental actions.

Q: *When Andre Green discusses primary narcissism, he seems in some ways to be thinking about aloneness.*

A: I am very pleased to hear my good friend Andre Green being referred to. I am not, however, convinced that the state of primary aloneness is equivalent to the narcissistic state of oneness. In my view, the narcissistic state of oneness is a memory of the infant's relation to the mother, of the foetus' relation to the uterus. Paradoxically, therefore, it is a oneness that is always based on twoness. This is an irony of the narcissistic state. Few are more dependent upon the other than the narcissist.

Q: *When does idiom arrive?*

A: Idiom is there before birth. In the course of psycho-development, it elaborates. In Freud's theory I don't think there is a specific way of addressing an organization of idiom at birth that evolves and elaborates throughout life. However, when I first became interested in this problem it seemed to me that the unconscious ego which Freud writes about, which in effect organizes repression and mental representation, is constructed in very early infancy.

I disagreed with the tendency to link the id with the true self and the ego with the false self. The unconscious ego is very close to the idea of the true self if we bear in mind inherited disposition and inherited organization.

Q: *How do you conceptualize the death drive?*

A: The death drive is the dismantling of the psychic apparatus. In the extreme form, the psyche is interpreted as the unconscious trace of a holding environment, and it must be destroyed in order to completely dismantle the subject.

Q: *What do you mean by timelessness?*

A: The infant needs the mother's capacity to contain him, to create reverie so that through the timelessness she establishes, the child feels held by life.

The timelessness that is characteristic of the primary process of the unconscious can be either a generative factor or a very disturbing one. We can say that there is an unconscious functioning which uses timelessness to allow for an undirected integration of all the factors in the person's experience. This is based on the mother's containment of the infant and her contribution to the experience that timelessness is to the benefit of both. However, if she does not establish a maternal containing function and facilitate reverie for herself and the infant, then the child feels lost in the unconscious, which is a form of madness.

Maternal time is very different from paternal time. In folklore, we speak of Father Time. An old man with the long beard. This father time represents the march of time, the passing of time. So, father time is movement through time, whilst maternal time is timelessness.

Millions of children exist in empty homes. With their parents out at work, they watch television or play alone. What does this imply? It means that no one is providing maternal time. Support for unconscious timelessness has disappeared. The internal space for reception of news from within the self has gone. In this situation there is no such thing here as solitude, only aloneness or isolation. Where timelessness was, there now is emptiness and despair.

Q: *What does Winnicott mean by stating that he wished he could be alive at his own death?*

A: I think this is a very moving passage. I discussed this at some length with Clare Winnicott. I think it is relevant here to bring in my concept of the 'unthought known': we can know something that has not yet been thought. This links too to Winnicott's idea of the inherited disposition that we all start with in life. It is my belief that we have a sense in us of the potential elaboration of our true self through time and human existence.

We can think of a human life as the gradual elaboration of the nuclei of our idiom. To be alive at our death means to have been imaginatively present in older age, to have been there, experiencing the final articulation of our potential.

17

Case Discussions

Q: *(following a clinical presentation): Do you think this hysterical patient, who is often psychotic, is still involved in object relating? And how does this differ from the borderline person?*

A: I think the analyst has a very specific aim in the presentation of her material. She organizes her psychic life through her dreams and her narratives in a cohesive manner, even if the details seem very crazy. She represents psychic content symbolically. She sucks her thumb, bangs her head, reads the newspaper; she shows, she demonstrates, she symbolizes. She presents mad scenes.

The borderline does not have a sense of addressing a specific person nor does he have the ability to organize mad scenes in this way. He does not have a sense of a receptive organized other; instead he projects psychic pain into the analyst without symbolically representing it. So projective identification is far more important for the borderline than for the hysteric.

In the countertransference when working with borderline patients, we can often find it very hard to think. There may be times when this patient functions in a borderline manner, but generally the therapist is able to think about her and can also feel affection and sympathy, which would not be so possible with a more borderline patient.

It is regrettable that the diagnosis of hysteria has more or less receded from the field of psychoanalysis.[1] When a patient

---

[1] I began to teach seminars on hysteria in the late 1980s and through the 1990s. The result was publication of *Hysteria* (Routledge, 1999).

Essential Aloneness. Christopher Bollas, Oxford University Press. © Christopher Bollas 2024.
DOI: 10.1093/oso/9780197683880.003.0017

guides us, leads us symbolically, no matter how crazy they may seem, I believe it is evidence of hysteria. Nowadays we seem to be reversing the great progress that Freud made in his discovery of this type of functioning. It can be especially hard to recognize a psychotic hysteric as they are now so often diagnosed as schizophrenic, but in diagnosing them as schizophrenic or borderline we are losing sight of the specificity of the hysteric.

With this patient the diagnosis of schizophrenia is, in my view, a catastrophe for her.

David

Q: *Would you comment on this morning's case presentation and the problems of working with the autistic child?*

A: When you reported the violent states of mind you experienced working with David,[2] you said, 'I felt he was communicating to me something very deep about his inner situation and his anxieties.' I would call this 'faith in the countertransference'. In other words, you have some faith that representation will be possible. Because there is nothing that he is doing to you here which suggests to me that he himself is giving you faith.

I think you simply have faith, and sometimes the very basis of faith is that there is no evidence whatsoever to support it. We can distinguish between faith and belief. In belief, usually there is evidence for believing in something. The strength of faith is the lack of any evidence to support it. In working with autistic children, or very disturbed children, I think we have faith but we don't have belief.

This child puts you inside the most wretched states that he himself has been in. The question here is whether he will cure you, and if he does cure you then your work will have come to

---

[2] The case presentation was not recorded and so is not presented here.

an end. There you are, alone in a dark room, curious and full of hate, and yet you have faith that he is telling you something. Will your faith be partly realized by this child?

Those of us who work with autistic children usually start with faith. When the treatment doesn't lead to visible or even invisible progress, we may lose faith in working with that patient and somebody else will need to take over.

You have described how your patient insisted on symmetrical activities: he wanted to sleep and therefore he wanted you to sleep with him, etcetera. But you don't describe your countertransference at this point. Since he was providing you with something to do, I would have thought that you must have felt at least a little bit happy that something seemed to be taking place inside the session. In other words, he was creating, on a symbolic level, a symbiotic relation to you. When it broke down, he became chaotic and overly anxious; then later you report that he began to construct things, to build things in the sessions. And again I think he does this in order to cure you.

The question is not 'Does this indicate that he is getting better?' Is that the essence of the session? No. The point is that you are getting better, moving from a countertransference of imprisonment, death, absence, and destruction into some creative partnership with the child.

So, it is his decision to allow you to be born, to be in a minimal partnership and to play with him in a minimal way. To me, this means that the child can symbolize the evolution of self, that he can believe in it, that he can symbolically represent it. And, in allowing you to breathe and to be alive and to not lose faith, he is certainly suggesting that he believes it is possible for this to happen in life. So I think we can look upon this situation with some cautious optimism.

Potential space, even if it is created in and of itself, cures nobody. Many great people, many brilliant artists who have made wonderful use of intermediate space, are deeply lost people. But

Winnicott's genius, I think, was to suggest that normal, sane people who were unable to make use of potential space or the intermediate area of experience were lacking in their personal creativity. He felt that when a patient came for analysis saying, 'I really have nothing to complain about. I'm very happy but I just don't feel creative,' this was an adequate reason for the person to seek an analysis. It was a particular sort of complaint, and it required a different approach to the analysis.

Anna

'Anna' is nine. She has been in three times weekly psychotherapy for two years. Anna was referred by her school because she was considered unteachable. Either silent in class and non-cooperative, she would decline visual contact with others or she would break out into manic hyperactivity becoming a blur of activity, accompanied by mentally confounding babble.

Academically, she was considerably behind in her writing skills and in her ability to narrate or represent what she had read and also what she thought.

She came from a distressed middle class family where the father was a distant figure in her infancy and early childhood. When she was three, Anna's mother gave birth and the sibling lived only six months. She got to know her sibling by visiting the grave with her mother.

Anna's mother became increasingly disturbed, the father lost his job, and although he picked up some work he was at home for long spells of time. The upside of this was that Anna turned to him for alternate mothering, and the evidence is that the father welcomed this opportunity to be useful.

The mother was a highly anxious, profoundly intrusive figure, always fretting about Anna. In the opening family meeting the mother interrupted her husband and Anna to finish sentences for them and to mangle their meaning. Some months after the therapy began, the hospital received a report on the family where it was disclosed that the mother had suffered psychotic episodes throughout Anna's childhood.

At the time of beginning therapy, Anna would wake very early in the morning and by mid-day would be exhausted and collapse into a nap. This pattern was disruptive to the family (and the school) and was a matter of some preoccupation to the world surrounding Anna.

[Now we turn to my commentary on the case presentation.]

In sessions Anna now and then plays with a few small wool-toy animals suitable for a three-year-old.

I will begin by discussing what I think Anna has organized into her personality. At the beginning of your work with her she would say:

> 'I draw, no wait, I draw'—repeatedly interrupting herself with incompatible assertions. This was her way of organizing the breaking up of continuity of being into her personality, transforming an environmental reality into a feature of her character.

By interrupting herself, *she* (not mother) recreates the interruption of her own existence. By transferring a relational dilemma into an intrapsychic one, she gives organization to chaos.

We note that she plays with toy animals, which seems a bit odd to some as she would seem to have outgrown that era.

Perhaps she inspires the toy animals to fill in the gaps created by her hesitations. Collecting toy animals might be a way of placing the toddler's self experiences into a physical-existential location.

When Anna breaks continuity in the sessions through hesitations and self interruptions—representing the maternal-existential pattern—the analyst's effort to fill in the space, in such moments, may re-present what Anna did as a child as she tried to offer something to the mother.

In that moment the analyst's comments are 'offerings'.

The analyst reports, however, that she feels her contributions are stupid and she feels helpless. They are not internalized and bounce off the patient.

Imagine that the analyst's experience matches that of the patient. Might the analyst's state echo Anna's experience of her mother? If so, then, unable to make a contribution to the mother's life, Anna passes this dilemma to the analyst who is subtly forced to live within it.

Further, as Anna always interrupts her own thinking to say, 'let me . . .' she shows how she cannot make a contribution to her own inner development, as something is stopping the 'me' from freedom of expression. Does she enact an intellectual impairment—interruption—that continues the pathology of her relation to her mother?

The analyst says that she would often find herself verbalizing the patient's mood. This is an important therapeutic action. Perhaps the analyst functions as a transformational object transforming moods and psychic states into language. In this way the analyst performs a function for the child, one the mother could not fulfil, and provides a living solution to Anna's dilemma.

As a result of this very important work, Anna rather launches herself into space. She flies around the room jumping all over the place. She cannot remember the analyst's name, and she has a loss of memory. The analyst reported this as confusing, but we may wonder if that is the intention. Through the child's imaginative and radical theatre, the mother-analyst cannot follow (or mirror) her.

Anna is free.

As importantly, having realized the transformational function of the analyst, it is now safe to become unintegrated.

The presence of this other, the analyst, ironically permits Anna to undergo the useful experience of 'no experience' of the object.

She needs to be in a state of no object cathexis. I believe she has no idea of what we could call *primary object usage*.

She does not know how to use the object. She only knows how to discharge instinctual and affective states into a void. Mental development at this point is precarious because at her age the superego can be so severe that the ego fragments in order to survive. When the superego is too harsh, it is not possible to maintain psychic integration.

Her early waking and afternoon sleepiness may have something to do with the terror of the superego, the attack which wakes her in the morning and the effort to defend by being dozy. Jumping around the room could be her positive use of nonsense.

She provides us with a clue when she draws a big grave and says there is a man in it, but he is only pretending to be dead. He has covered himself with paper just to play a trick. Then she draws a girl coming out of the paper and says she is alive. She says her mother is there—crying; whereupon Anna becomes very scared.

We know that she has had a good relationship with her father, more or less, and that he mothered her after the death of her sibling. The grave represents many things, including the death of the mother. But inside the death of the mother is the emerging and arising presence of the father. Out of death—which combines the loss of a sibling and the loss of mother, a girl emerges.

We see the cure of representation. The child imagines a new beginning, well concealed in the apparent nonsense of her behaviour.

We know that her reorganization of self is a result of being 'born again' out of the relation to the father. And the fact that she is born out of paper, that she comes out of paper that covers the father, suggests to me (because of course we draw on paper, we make words on paper) that her identity comes out of that phase of her life that follows the acquisition of language. Her problems at school have to do with writing and the problem of representation. (She refuses.)

Even though the turn to father was an intelligent move on the part of her ego, what was adaptive and integrative at that time in her life becomes a problem soon afterwards. Indeed, she must break down this type of birth: coming from the father. Perhaps this is why she must tear pieces of paper, because she is trying to somehow tear apart the false origin of her identity being born out of the father. At the same time, after telling this story of her birth, she says that she feels her being is 'stragic', a neologism which she clarified means strange, tired and tragic. As I understand it, I think she says, 'but if I am not born out of my father, how can I be born out of my mother, because this is where I should have been asked to be born.'

There is a further irony because many times she refers to 'the story', to family history, because this tragic story—of great despair, near death, separation, abandonment, and madness—has dominated her life. I think that she is also seeking to be free not simply of identification with the mother—she does not wish to go inside the mother—but wants to free herself from imprisonment in the family story.

In the beginning of one session, she brings a comic book into the room and is silent for fifteen minutes. The silence seems to have a very positive function. She shows pictures of the grave and then a chapter from a book, *Little Women Grow*, and refers to a little girl standing by the graveyard. The analyst says the little girl has suffered a serious loss. And of course this is right, but she looks amazed at the analyst. I don't think she is amazed, because I think she knows this connection. It makes sense to her, and the work that has been achieved in this regard is very important.

Why her surprise?

That the other should know this.

The surprise is that she is just becoming known and knowable.

She reads another story and becomes distracted, and she moves around a lot then because she does not want to be trapped inside this story anymore, because the story has become the equivalent of the mother's body and the mother's person.

But having now established that the other does know her, there is no need for her to remain attached to miming the story of her life.

On reflection, it is likely that our understanding of our patients—especially our verbal representations of the mother or the father—may become the presence of the mother or the father. And after a while, patients no longer wish to be inside this presence.

So in a remarkable moment, the analyst says that Anna looks frantically for a pencil in the toy box, finds a can of dried up glue, turns it over on the table, and with a little brush divides the larger pieces from the crumbs with a movement that reminds the analyst of a jeweller choosing the best stones. As the analyst thinks this, Anna says 'I divide the jewels.' So in other words, she does not want any more representations of the sad little girl in relation to the tragic mother or in relation to the tragic father. This feels like a trap: the trap she's always been in and one she has to break out of in the session.

She accomplishes this by running around and around. She breaks up the session, moving objects in front of her like pieces of glue. The analyst thinks it's like jewellery and the patient says it. In that moment they have found contact with each other at the level of nonsense not of narrative, but through object relating. It is an irony of clinical work that we must continue to reach our patients through interpretations, and I think the interpretations of the analyst are very similar to the one I would be giving. And in fact we learned a lot from the patients' need through their disturbance of our interpretation.

I would like to draw attention to another aspect of this clinical work because the analyst is analysing object relating, the child's relation to the animals. I think this is very important, because it helps us to understand why this patient is responding so positively to the analyst. There is a difference between analysing object relationships and their projection of internal objects onto the analyst. Of course both are important, but it is necessary to know the difference. An analysis of object relationships involves interpretation in the here and now: of the patient's feelings toward the analyst and interrelationships and analysis of internal object relations that involves the explication of unconscious fantasies. Analysis of internal object relations involves a very different mental process in the patient than analysis of projective identification in object relating.

It seems Anna feels as if her whole self, her body self is present in the sessions. She says that that night they are going out for pizza, and tomorrow there will be a party at school, and she puffs and touches her breast and belly and sighs heavily.

Puffing, showing her chest, sighing heavily, draws attention to her body which she knows grows by virtue of eating and taking something in. The stomach is important, the breasts are important, respiratory activity is important. It is as if she is bringing the body to the mother in the transference: the mother who has never seen (appreciated) this body. At this moment perhaps we see a good regressed state of the infant in front of mother. She takes a ball from the box and says, 'let's play' and throws the ball violently at the analyst.

At an unconscious level perhaps she is taking what she created through the pizza. It is in the belly and in the breast, forms an object that is not hallucination, but real, and says something like the following: 'I take in, I've got something in, I move it out . . . you've got it.'

Might she be trying to find a way to create objects that have a mixture of internal projective elements and external reality to break into relation to Mama? But then she seems to feel that she must start to think, that she has to start organizing in the mind, so she goes to a blackboard and tries to divide it and writes names. She forgets her own name and becomes very confused. The analyst comments that Anna is presenting a pathology that had not happened for a long time—forgetting the names—but perhaps the patient is showing us why and how her pathology emerges. And she does show the problem, just as she tries to form a relation between psychic reality and external reality, between internal and external, between pizza, body, and ball.

Puff, it's gone and she's 'in' in the mind. She forgets names, she loses contact with reality. This may be her way of saying 'this is where my illness comes from.' Now of course, as no doubt most of us would, because this is before the holidays, the analyst believes the patient is communicating something about the shock of separation and therefore tries to address it from that point of view. But the patient starts to laugh, and the words she writes are nonsense words which make nonsense of interpretations.

Then she takes the same ball, throws it high up in the air, making it impossible for the analyst to catch it. And the analyst starts to feel angry as if forced into too much engagement, but has revenge because the analyst wins. Actually in this game between the two, it is more like the relation of the infant to the mother, where the Mama is always trying to deal with exhaustion and fatigue but in the end, if it comes down to a battle of strength, Mum is going to win. I emphasize this because I think it is the quality of the object relationship that is one of the curative factors in this girl's treatment.

Perhaps Anna is saying: *'thoughts come from objects.'* In order for thoughts to be interpreted, primary objects must be integrated. So the ball becomes what we could call a 'thought-object' or an 'object-thought', and it is this double aspect of the ball that makes it such an important feature of the exchange.

At this point in the treatment she is beginning to discover the pleasures of engagement with the analyst. And this has to do with the pleasure of instinctual life, which of course involves excitement and over-excitement and triumph and all of that, but it is not discharge phenomenon. She is not discharging. If this were a discharge phenomenon she would throw the ball at the wall, or she would not even pick up a ball at all. She would just discharge instinct. She throws the ball *at* the analyst. So we can speak of instinctual life within an object relationship.

At the very end she plays better than the analyst, and she wins after having felt a depression over the possibility of losing. She says 'I play to win', and she pants and acts as if she is hot. So one can say that in the course of this object relationship, in which objects are exchanged, she has experienced something like ordinary depression and ordinary mania.

What has she done? She knows there is a holiday, and she knows there is a separation. So when she says, 'I play to win', she may be illustrating that she can deal with the absence because she is discovering mastery of self in relation to objects and to others. At the very end of the session, there is a moment's confusion with the key and the lock, but her last words—'I play to win'—suggests there will be more material in this analysis.

Anna is feeding from an internal breast (the introjected analyst) and is now able to get fat inside. She will generate her own psychic life.

Winnicott Bibliography

Babies and their Mothers. London, Free Association Books, 1988.
The Child, the Family, and the Outside World. London, Penguin, 1964.
Deprivation and Delinquency. London and New York, Tavistock, 1984.
The Family and Individual Development. London, Tavistock, 1965.
Holding and Interpretation. London, The Hogarth Press,1986.
Home is Where We Start From. London, Penguin, 1986.
Human Nature. London, Free Association Books,1988.
The Maturational Process and the Facilitating Environment. London, Hogarth, 1972.
The Piggle. London, Hogarth, 1978.
Playing and Reality. London, Tavistock, 1971.
Psychoanalytic Explorations. London, Karnac Books, 1989.
Talking to Parents. New York, Addison-Wesley, 1993.
Through Paediatrics to Psycho-Analysis. London, Hogarth, 1975.

Works on Winnicott

Essential reading

Jan Abram, *The Language of Winnicott.* London, Karnac, 1996.
Adam Phillips, *Winnicott.* London, Fontana, 1988.

Further reading

D.W. Winnicott, *Collected Works*, eds. Lesley Caldwell and Helen Taylor Robinson. Oxford, Oxford University Press, 2018.

Index

For the benefit of digital users, indexed terms that span two pages (e.g., 52–53) may, on occasion, appear on only one of those pages.